D058260?

Great Escapes
Africa

Texts by Shelley-Maree Cassidy   *Edited by* Angelika Taschen

Great Escapes
Africa

TASCHEN

HONG KONG KÖLN LONDON LOS ANGELES MADRID PARIS TOKYO

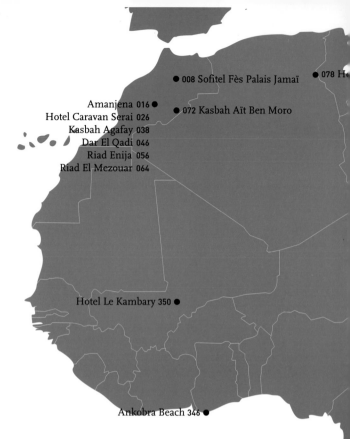

All I wanted to do now was get back to Africa. We had not left it,
yet, but when I would wake in the night I would lie, listening,
homesick for it already.

Ernest Hemingway, *Green Hills of Africa*, 1994

Kensingt

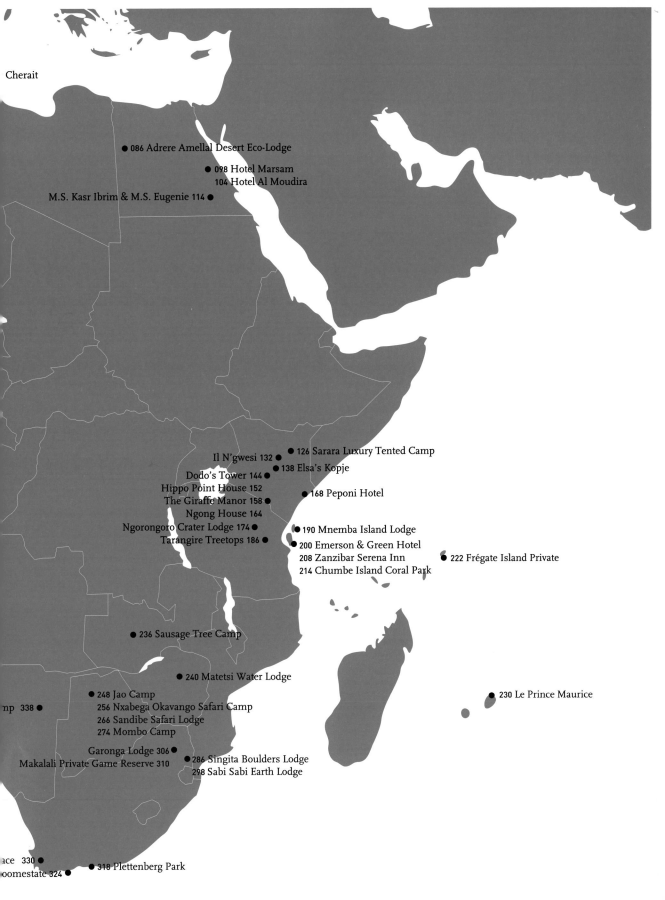

Cherait

Contents   Inhalt   Sommaire

Price categories:		Preiskategorien:		Catégories de prix:	
$	up to 150 US$	$	bis 150 US$	$	jusqu'à 150 US$
$$	up to 250 US$	$$	bis 250 US$	$$	jusqu'à 250 US$
$$$	up to 450 US$	$$$	bis 450 US$	$$$	jusqu'à 450 US$
$$$$	over 450 US$	$$$$	über 450 US$	$$$$	plus de 450 US$

Medieval mystique...

Sofitel Fès Palais Jamaï, Fès

Sofitel Fès Palais Jamaï, Fes

Medieval mystique

Founded in the 8th century, Fez is the most beautiful and well-preserved medieval city in the Islamic world. For many centuries, it was the commercial, cultural and religious heart of Morocco. Now, with its many fine mosques and palaces, flourishing souks and bazaars, Fez still has the mystique of an ancient Arab capital.

The historic Palais Jamaï Hotel is in the centre of the old city, overlooking the valley of Fez. Built in 1879 by the Grand Vizir to the Sultan, it typifies traditional Moorish architecture. The lavish rooms are decorated in Moroccan cedar and painted with classic geometric motifs. Bounded by an impressive Andalusian garden with several fountains and terraces, the hotel is a peaceful retreat, despite its proximity to the hustle and bustle of the Medina – the walled city.

The fascinating sights of Fez are best visited on foot. Palais Jamaï guests can walk down twisting narrow alleys lined with tiny shops selling carpets, sequined slippers, fabrics, leatherwork, jewellery and spices. The alleys also lead to some of Fez's most famous monuments, such as the great Kairaouiine Mosque, the focus of religious life in Morocco.

Book to pack: "Morocco" by Pierre Loti

Sofitel Fès Palais Jamaï

Bab Guissa

3000 Fes

Morocco

Tel: + 212 (35) 63 43 31

Fax: + 212 (35) 63 50 96

E-mail: H2141@accor.com

Website: www.sofitel.com

www.great-escapes-hotels.com

DIRECTIONS	15 km/9 m from Fez Saïss Airport and 5 km/3 m from the railway station of Fez
RATES	$$
ROOMS	123 rooms, most of them with balcony, and 19 suites, overlooking either the mountains, the Medina or the gardens
FOOD	Refined and authentic Moroccan cuisine as well as international dishes in a casual yet chic atmosphere
HISTORY	Converted into a hotel in the 1930s, it was extended in the 1970s, and renovated in 1999
X-FACTOR	Moorish style in a great location, with a large swimming pool

Mittelalterliche Mystik

Fez, gegründet im achten Jahrhundert, ist die schönste und best erhaltene mittelalterliche Stadt der islamischen Welt. Jahrhunderte lang stellte sie das kommerzielle, kulturelle und religiöse Herzstück Marokkos dar. Mit seinen vielen fein gearbeiteten Moscheen und Palästen, seinen florierenden Souks und Bazaren, haftet Fez auch heute noch die Mystik einer arabischen Hauptstadt längst verflossener Zeiten an. Das historische Hotel Palais Jamaï liegt im Zentrum der Altstadt über dem Tal von Fez. Es wurde im Jahre 1879 vom Großwesir für den Sultan erbaut und verkörpert den typisch traditionellen maurischen Baustil. Die aufwändigen Räume sind mit marokkanischem Zedernholz getäfelt und mit klassischen geometrischen Motiven bemalt. Obwohl das Hotel nicht weit entfernt ist vom geschäftigen Treiben der Medina, dem Teil der Altstadt, der innerhalb der Stadtmauern liegt, stellt es, umsäumt von einem bemerkenswerten, andalusischen Garten mit mehreren Springbrunnen und Terrassen, einen friedlicher Zufluchtsort dar. Die faszinierenden Sehenswürdigkeiten von Fez erkundet man am besten zu Fuß. Gäste des Palais Jamaïs haben die Möglichkeit gewundene, schmale Gassen hinabzusteigen, vorbei an winzigen Läden, die Teppiche, paillettenbesetzte Schuhe, Stoffe, Lederwaren, Schmuck oder Gewürze verkaufen. Außerdem führen die Gässchen hinab zu einigen der bekanntesten Monumente in Fez, wie beispielsweise zur berühmten Kairaouiine Moschee, dem Brennpunkt des religiösen Lebens in Marokko.

Buchtipp: »Im Zeichen der Sahara« von Pierre Loti

Mystique médiéval

Fondée au VIIIe siècle, Fès est la cité médiévale la plus belle et la mieux préservée du monde islamique. Cœur commercial, culturel et religieux du Maroc pendant bien des siècles, Fès conserve, grâce à ses nombreux et superbes palais et mosquées et à ses *souks* et ses bazars florissants, l'atmosphère mystique d'une antique capitale arabe. L'historique hôtel Palais Jamaï se trouve au centre de la vieille ville et donne sur la vallée de Fès. Construit en 1879 par le Grand Vizir du Sultan, son architecture est caractéristique du style maure traditionnel. Ses luxueuses chambres sont décorées de cèdre marocain et ornées de motifs géométriques classiques. Entouré d'un magnifique jardin andalou agrémenté de plusieurs fontaines et terrasses, l'hôtel est une paisible retraite malgré la proximité de la médina, la cité fortifiée, où règne l'effervescence. Le meilleur moyen d'apprécier les sites fascinants de Fès est de les visiter à pied. Ainsi, les résidents du Palais Jamaï descendront le long de ruelles étroites et sinueuses bordées de petites boutiques vendant tapis, pantoufles à sequins, étoffes, articles en cuir, bijoux et épices. Ces mêmes ruelles les conduiront à quelques-uns des plus célèbres monuments de Fès, notamment la grande mosquée Qarawiyyine, centre névralgique de la vie religieuse au Maroc.

Livre à emporter : « Au Maroc » de Pierre Loti

ANREISE	15 km vom Flughafen Fez Saïss Airport und 5 km von dem Bahnhof in Fez entfernt
PREIS	$$
ZIMMER	123 Zimmer, die meisten davon mit Balkon, sowie 19 Suiten mit Blick auf die Berge, die Medina oder die Gärten
KÜCHE	Verfeinerte und authentisch marokkanische Küche, sowie internationale Gerichte in lockerer und dennoch eleganter Atmosphäre
GESCHICHTE	In den 30er Jahren zum Hotel umfunktioniert, erweitert in den 70ern und 1999 renoviert
X-FAKTOR	Maurischer Stil in großartiger Lage

ACCÈS	À 15 km de l'aéroport de Fès Saïss et à 5 Km de la gare
PRIX	$$
CHAMBRES	123, dont la plupart avec balcon, et 19 suites donnant sur les montagnes, la Médina ou les jardins
RESTAURATION	Cuisine marocaine authentique et raffinée et plats du monde entier à déguster dans une ambiance à la fois simple et chic
HISTOIRE	Transformé en hôtel dans les années 30, le bâtiment a été agrandi dans les années 70 et rénové en 1999
LES « PLUS »	Style mauresque dans un emplacement de toute beauté avec une grande priscine

A star is born...
Amanjena, near Marrakech

A star is born

Can there be a mirage in an oasis? Such a stunning scene
in the desert is more often than not a mere vision. This
could be a film set: a Hollywood dream of a Moorish palace.
But the glamorous scene is real, not an illusion.

This serene place is the sumptuous Moroccan resort of
Amanjena; framed by pink tinged walls, set among palms
and olive trees, with a dramatic backdrop of snow-capped
mountains that glitter in the sun and turn roseate at day's
end. Though it is new, it has a timeless feel. The pictures of
this lavish location need few words; they show that luxury is
on offer here. There is the luxury of space; of calm; of rest;
and privacy. You can stay secluded within the walls of your
own domain, shutting out the rest of the world, if you so
choose. Each pavilion has a courtyard and dining room of
its own; some have private pools.

The focal point is a great pool, sixty square metres in size.
Termed a basin, it was traditionally used to collect water
from the mountains. Here its purpose is just a decorative
one. Its tranquil surface reflects the sky by day; by night,
it mirrors the lights of lanterns, candles and the stars.

All the vigour of Marrakech is just a short drive away, as are
Berber villages and beaches. Some will give thanks that two
of the best golf courses are near this peaceful paradise.

Book to pack: "The Sheltering Sky" by Paul Bowles

Amanjena
Route de Ouarzazate, km 12
Marrakech
Morocco
Tel: + 212 (24) 403 353
Fax: + 212 (24) 403 477
E-mail: amanjena@amanresorts.com
Website:
www.amanresorts.com
www.great-escapes-hotels.com

DIRECTIONS	A 20-minute drive north from Marrakech's Menara airport
RATES	$$$$
ROOMS	6 two storey maisons, 34 pavilions
FOOD	Moroccan, European and Thai tastes opulently catered
HISTORY	Opened in 2000, the first Aman resort on the African continent
X-FACTOR	A fabulous fantasy retreat. Back to the real world at the end

A star is born

Kann es in einer Oase eine Fata Morgana geben? Denn man könnte meinen, dass ein solch überwältigender Anblick eigentlich nichts als bloße Einbildung sein kann. Dieser Ort könnte Drehort für einen Film sein: ein Traum von einem maurischen Palast à la Hollywood. Doch dieser zauberhafte Schauplatz ist keine Illusion, sondern Wirklichkeit.

Die Rede ist von dem opulenten marokkanischen Amanjena-Resort, – mit rosé-mellierten Wänden befindet er sich zwischen Palmen und Olivenbäumen vor einer spektakulären Kulisse von schneebedeckten Bergen, die in der Sonne glitzern und sich blutrot färben, wenn der Tag zur Neige geht. Obwohl die Anlage neu ist, scheint sie zeitlos zu sein. Die Bilder dieser üppigen Anlage sprechen für sich, sie zeigen, dass hier der Luxus zu Hause ist. Sei es der Luxus, viel Platz zu haben, der Luxus der Ruhe, der Entspannung oder der Ungestörtheit. Wer möchte, kann zurückgezogen in seinem privaten Bereich bleiben und sich vom Rest der Welt abschotten. Jeder Pavillon hat einen eigenen Hof und ein eigenes Speisezimmer, manche verfügen über Privatpools. Mittelpunkt bildet ein großartiges Wasserbecken mit einer Fläche von vierundsechzig Quadratmetern. Seine Bezeichnung Bassin deutet an, dass derartige Becken traditionellerweise genutzt wurden, um das Wasser zu speichern das aus den Bergen kam. In diesem Falle dient es jedoch ausschließlich dekorativen Zwecken. Am Tage spiegelt seine ruhige Oberfläche den Himmel wider, in der Nacht wirft es das Licht von Laternen, Kerzen und Sternen zurück.

Das pulsierende Leben in Marrakesch, Berberdörfer und Strände sind nur eine kurze Autofahrt weit entfernt. So mancher wird sich freuen, dass auch zwei der besten Golfplätze ganz in der Nähe dieses friedlichen Paradieses liegen.

Buchtipp: »Himmel über der Wüste« von Paul Bowles

Une étoile est née

Les mirages existent-ils aussi dans les oasis ?

Car on pourrait penser qu'une vue aussi grandiose est l'effet d'une illusion. Un tel lieu pourrait servir de décor de cinéma : un palais maure comme on en rêve à Hollywood. Non, le cadre grandiose qui s'offre à vos yeux est bien réel.

Ce lieu serein, c'est la somptueuse station touristique marocaine d'Amanjena. Encadrée de murs aux tons roses, située au milieu de palmiers et d'oliviers, elle a pour spectaculaire toile de fond des montagnes enneigées qui resplendissent au soleil et se teintent de rouge sang le soir venu. L'hôtel est récent, mais il inspire un sentiment d'éternité. Les photos de cet endroit fastueux parlent d'elles-mêmes : le mot-clé est ici le luxe, un luxe d'espace, de calme, de repos et d'intimité. Chaque pavillon ayant sa propre cour et sa propre salle à manger, et certains disposant même d'une piscine privée, vous pouvez rester à l'abri des murs de votre domaine et oublier le monde extérieur si vous le souhaitez.

Le point central d'Amanjena est un grand bassin de soixante mètres carrés, traditionnellement utilisé pour recueillir l'eau des montagnes. Sa fonction est aujourd'hui décorative. Le jour, sa surface tranquille réfléchit le ciel et la nuit, elle reflète la lumière des étoiles et celle des bougies brûlant dans les lanternes.

L'effervescence et l'énergie de Marrakech ne sont qu'à quelques minutes en voiture, tout comme les villages berbères et les plages. Certains seront ravis d'apprendre que deux des meilleurs terrains de golf du monde sont à proximité de ce paisible paradis.

Livre à emporter : « Un Thé au Sahara » de Paul Bowles

ANREISE	20-minütige Fahrt nördlich vom Flughafen Marrakesch
PREIS	$$$$
ZIMMER	6 Häuser, 34 Pavillons
KÜCHE	Aufwändig zubereitete marokkanische, europäische und thailändische Gerichte
GESCHICHTE	Der erste Aman-Resort auf dem afrikanischen Kontinent, eröffnet im Jahr 2000
X-FAKTOR	Märchenhafter Zufluchtsort mit anschließender Rückkehr in die Wirklichkeit

ACCÈS	À 20 minutes au nord de l'aéroport de Marrakech en voiture
PRIX	$$$$
CHAMBRES	6 maisons, 34 pavillons
RESTAURATION	Succulents menus marocains, européens et thaïlandais
HISTOIRE	Ouvert en 2000, il s'agit du premier hôtel Aman du continent africain
LES « PLUS »	Retraite de rêve. Le retour à la réalité est difficile

Courtyard cloister...
Hotel Caravan Serai, near Marrakech

Hotel Caravan Serai,
near Marrakech

Courtyard cloister

It seems that the very first hotels were formed to cater for tour groups. Travelling in convoy has been a custom for a very long time. It started when merchants banded together for safety in numbers as they moved through unknown territory seeking to trade their goods. Places for them to rest their animals and themselves en route sprang up – the first hotels, or, as they were called, caravanserai.

The lovely old Persian word has been applied to this present-day hotel, but one that is, luckily, not for a large group. The CaravanSerai is a place to rest, yet far more stylish than the early ones would have been. Such a romantic setting would tempt most travellers to just stay put, rather than go on with the rest of their trip. From the tower at its gate to the long flowing banners that frame the entrance, there is a real sense of theatre at play. "To travel hopefully is better than to arrive" is not true of here; the result of arrival is to be well content with the handsome scene that first meets the eye. Then, more unfolds; a sequence of courtyards and pools, alcoves and arches; all within the high walls. Their thickness mutes sound, adding to the effect of quiet inside. Dramatic views are on show from the roof terraces. On the horizon, a line of jagged mountain peaks; and nearer, across the date groves, the landmark minaret of the Koutibia mosque gleams gold in the sun.

Book to pack: "For Bread Alone" by Mohamed Choukri

Hotel Caravan Serai	
264 Ouled Ben Rahmoune	
40000 Marrakech	
Morocco	
Tel: + 212 (24) 300 302	
Fax: + 212 (24) 300 262	
Website: www.hotel-caravanserai.com	
www.great-escapes-hotels.com	

DIRECTIONS	11 km/7 m north of Marrakech, in the village of Ouled Ben Rahmoun
RATES	$$
ROOMS	17 including two suites with private pools
FOOD	Moroccan staples – tagine, couscous, village-baked breads; and European options – club sandwiches, pasta, salads
HISTORY	Opened in 2002, complete with a hammam and masseuse
X-FACTOR	Simple serene haven for a few, yet close to the bustle of Marrakech

Klösterliche Frieden

Die ersten Hotels wurden für Karawanen errichtet, die auf der Durchreise waren, denn lange Zeit über war es üblich im Konvoi zu reisen. Um der Sicherheit willen schlossen sich Händler in großen Zahlen zusammen, wenn sie durch unbekanntes Gebiet zogen, um ihre Waren an den Mann zu bringen. So entstanden entlang der Routen Orte, an welchen sie sich und ihren Herden eine Ruhepause gönnen konnten – die ersten Hotels wenn man so will – oder, wie man sie damals nannte, Karawanserai.

Jenes bezaubernde alte persische Wort hat diesem modernen Hotel, das im Gegensatz dazu glücklicherweise nicht dafür ausgelegt ist, große Reisegruppen zu beherbergen, seinen Namen gegeben. Auch diese »CaravanSerai« ist ein Ort der Rast – doch wesentlich stilvoller als seine frühen Vorgänger. Ein derart romantisches Plätzchen hätte die meisten Reisenden wohl dazu verführt, länger hier zu verweilen, und reichlich wenig Ansporn geboten, die Reise fortzusetzen. Mit dem Turm an seinem Tor und den langen, fließenden Fahnen, die den Eingang umrahmen, entsteht ein Hauch von theatralischer Bühnenatmosphäre. Die Redensart »hoffnungsfroh Reisen ist besser als anzukommen« trifft hier überhaupt nicht zu. Wer hier ankommt, den belohnt schon ein erster Blick auf dieses schöne Ambiente, das sich dem Betrachter nach und nach weiter eröffnet, wenn er die vielen aneinandergereihten Höfe und Wasserbecken, Alkoven und Bögen erblickt, die alle innerhalb der hohen Mauern liegen. Die dicken Mauern dämpfen die Geräusche und verstärken so die Stille, die in ihrem Innern herrscht. Von der Dachterrasse aus bietet sich eine dramatisch schöne Aussicht. Am Horizont zeichnet sich die zerklüftete Silhouette einer Gipfelkette ab und in weniger weiter Entfernung, jenseits der Dattelhaine glänzt das Minarett von Koutibia, das berühmte Wahrzeichen der Gegend, golden in der Sonne.

Buchtipp: »Das nackte Brot. Ein autobiographischer Roman und fünfzehn Erzählungen« von Mohamed Choukri

Une intimité de cloître

Il semble que les tout premiers hôtels furent créés pour accueillir les caravanes. Se déplacer en convoi est une coutume qui existe depuis fort longtemps. Tout a commencé avec les marchands qui, par mesure de sécurité, voyageaient en groupe lorsqu'ils se rendaient dans des contrées inconnues pour vendre leurs marchandises.

Des auberges commencèrent alors à s'édifier le long de la route pour leur permettre de se reposer et de laisser souffler leurs montures. Les premiers hôtels, ou comme on les appelait à l'époque, les caravansérails, étaient nés.

Ce joli mot du persan ancien a donné son nom à un hôtel moderne, heureusement non prévu pour accueillir autant de monde que ses homonymes du passé. Le « CaravanSerai » est également un endroit fait pour se reposer, mais son élégance surpasse de beaucoup celle de ses ancêtres et son ambiance romantique aurait plutôt tendance à inciter la plupart des hôtes à rester au lieu de continuer leur voyage. Avec sa tour à l'entrée et ses longues bannières flottant au vent qui décorent le hall, l'hôtel est très théâtral et la satisfaction que procure la beauté du cadre dès le premier instant dément le proverbe « mieux vaut voyager plein d'espoir que d'arriver au but ». L'hôtel recèle bien d'autres trésors : une succession de cours et de bassins, d'alcôves et d'arcs, derrière des hauts murs dont l'épaisseur étouffe les sons et ajoute à la tranquillité du lieu. Les terrasses du toit offrent une vue spectaculaire sur le paysage environnant : un horizon hérissé de pics montagneux et, plus près, au-delà des palmeraies, le célèbre minaret de la mosquée Koutoubia étincelant comme de l'or au soleil.

Livre à emporter : « Le Pain nu » de Mohamed Choukri

ANREISE	11 km nördlich von Marrakesch, in dem Dorf Ouled Ben Rahmoun
PREIS	$$
ZIMMER	17, inklusive zweier Suiten mit Privatpool
KÜCHE	Einfache marokkanische Gerichte – Tagine, Couscous und Brot aus dem Dorf; ebenso gibt es auch europäische Gerichte, Sandwichs, Nudelgerichte und Salate
GESCHICHTE	Eröffnet im Jahr 2002, ausgestattet mit Hammam und Masseurin
X-FAKTOR	Ein einfacher und freundlicher kleiner Zufluchtsort, dennoch in der Nähe vom geschäftigen Treiben in Marrakesch

ACCÈS	À 11 km au nord de Marrakech, dans le village d'Ouled Ben Rahmoun
PRIX	$$
CHAMBRES	17, dont deux suites disposent d'une piscine privée
RESTAURATION	Cuisine simple et typiquement marocaine (tajine, couscous, pain traditionnel) et choix de plats européens (sandwiches mixtes, pâtes, salades)
HISTOIRE	Ouvert en 2002 ; hammam et massages
LES « PLUS »	Retraite tranquille réservée à quelques privilégiés, tout près du tourbillon d'activité de Marrakech

Fort Marrakech

Kasbah Agafay, near Marrakech

Fort Marrakech

Once a derelict hilltop fort owned by a holy man, this
landmark building is now in the hands of a visionary
designer. In a dramatic tribute to Morocco's architectural
heritage, the traditional Berber mud fort has been trans-
formed into a stunning and exclusive retreat, with pano-
ramic views over olive groves, desert hills and the snow-
capped Atlas Mountains.

Inside the massive terraced ramparts of the Kasbah Agafay
are spacious suites, decorated in contemporary style and
surrounded by terraced gardens and traditional courtyards –
riads. A traditional hammam – steam bath – and meditation
cave are pleasurable elements of this serene haven. You
can choose to spend a night or more in a Berber tent,
sumptuously furnished with antiques and traditional textiles,
enjoying a candlelit supper under the starry sky, amidst
palm groves. Daylight excursions include tours of Marrakech
palaces and the souk, camel and horse treks, and visits to
local Berber villages to learn about their traditional cooking,
music and culture.

Outside the city in a unique desert setting, away from
the noise and bustle of the marketplace, but close enough
to visit, this idyllic bolthole offers an authentic Kasbah
experience.

Book to pack: "Mother Comes of Age" by Driss Chraibi

Kasbah Agafay
Route de Guemassa, km 20
40000 Marrakech Medina
Morocco
Tel: + 212 (24) 368 600
Fax: + 212 (24) 420 970
E-mail: kasbahagafay@menara.ma
Website: www.kasbahagafay.com
www.great-escapes-hotels.com

DIRECTIONS	15 km/9 m west from Marrakech's Menara airport, 20 km/12 m from the city centre
RATES	$$$
ROOMS	14 suites, 4 luxury tented suites
FOOD	Moroccan, Berber and international cuisine
HISTORY	Re-opened in December 2000 after an intensive three year restoration programme
X-FACTOR	Stunning desert setting and style and a large mosaic tiled swimming pool

Fort Marrakesch

Während dieses charakteristische Gebäude einst eine heruntergekommene Festung und im Besitz eines heiligen Mannes war, gehört es heute einem visionären Designer. Auf eindrucksvolle Weise wurde dem marokkanischen Architekturerbe Tribut gezollt, als diese traditionelle Berber-Lehmfestung in einen überwältigend schönen und exklusiven Zufluchtsort mit Panoramablick über Olivenhaine, Wüstenhügel und das Atlas Gebirge mit seinen schneebedeckten Gipfeln umgewandelt wurde.

In den massiven terrassenartigen Wällen der Kasbah Agafay verbergen sich geräumige Suiten – ausgestattet in zeitgenössischem Stil und umgeben von Terrassengärten und landestypischen Höfen – riads. Ein traditionelles Hammam – Dampfbad – und eine Meditationshöhle sind angenehme Elemente in dieser unbeschwerten Oase. Auf Wunsch können Sie eine oder mehrere Nächte in einem mit kostbaren Antiquitäten und Textilien ausgestatteten Berberzelt zubringen und bei Kerzenschein ein Abendessen unter Sternenhimmel in einem Palmenhain genießen.

Zu den möglichen Tagesexkursionen gehören Touren zu Palästen und dem Souk (Markt) in Marrakesch, Kamel- und Pferdeausritte, sowie Besuche in nahegelegenen Berberdörfern, wo man Wissenswertes über deren Kochgewohnheiten, Musik und Kultur erfahren kann. Außerhalb der Stadt und weit entfernt vom Lärm und der Betriebsamkeit des Marktes, und dennoch nah genug für einen Besuch, bietet dieses idyllische Versteck ein authentisches Kasbah Erlebnis.

Buchtipp: »Die Zivilisation, Mutter!« von Driss Chraïbi

Fort Marrakech

La Kasbah Agafay, remarquable construction érigée au sommet d'une colline, appartenait autrefois à un religieux. Jadis en ruine, ce fort berbère traditionnel est passé aux mains d'un créateur visionnaire. Aujourd'hui retraite spectaculaire et luxueuse rendant hommage à l'héritage architectural marocain, il domine un paysage d'oliveraies et de collines désertiques et permet d'admirer les sommets enneigés de l'Atlas.

À l'intérieur, les immenses remparts en terrasses accueillent des suites spacieuses de style contemporain cernées de jardins également en terrasses et de cours typiques, les *riads*. Le *hammam* (bain de vapeur) traditionnel et la grotte de méditation sont deux agréables composants de ce havre de paix. Vous pourrez passer une nuit ou plus sous une tente berbère somptueusement décorée d'antiquités et d'étoffes traditionnelles. Le dîner, éclairé aux chandelles sous un ciel étoilé, est servi au milieu des palmeraies. Les excursions de jour comprennent des randonnées à dos de chameau et de cheval. Vous pourrez également visiter les palais et le *souk* de Marrakech ainsi que les villages berbères dont vous découvrirez la cuisine, la musique et la culture traditionnelles.

Situé en dehors de la ville dans un paysage désertique unique, loin du bruit et de l'effervescence de la place du marché, mais assez près pour visiter, ce refuge idyllique vous permettra de faire l'expérience de la vie dans une authentique casbah.

Livre à emporter : « La civilisation, ma Mère ! » de Driss Chraïbi

ANREISE	15 km westlich vom Menara Flughafen bei Marrakesch entfernt, 20 km von der Stadtmitte
PREIS	$$$
ZIMMER	14 Suiten, 4 Luxus-Zeltsuiten
KÜCHE	Marokkanisch, Berberspezialitäten und internationale Küche
GESCHICHTE	Nach aufwändiger, dreijährige Restaurierung, im Dezember 2000 wiedereröffnet
X-FAKTOR	Umwerfende Wüstenatmosphäre und ein großer mit Mosaiken ausgelegter Swimming Pool

ACCÈS	À 15 Km à l'ouest de l'aéroport de Menara près de Marrakech, à 20 km du centre-ville
PRIX	$$$
CHAMBRES	14 suites, 4 tentes aménagées en suites luxueuses
RESTAURATION	Cuisine marocaine, berbère et internationale
HISTOIRE	Rouvert en décembre 2000 après une restauration intensive de trois ans
LES « PLUS »	Style et cadre désertique impressionnants ainsi qu'une grande piscine carrelée en mosaïque

A cosmic retreat...
Dar El Qadi, Marrakech

Dar El Qadi, Marrakech

A cosmic retreat

If you have learned the constellations and the stars in the sky, then wherever you are in the World you will never be lost. They are a "guiding light in the canopy of the heavens." By knowing the stars, you can tell what latitude you are at, find where north is, and thus all the other directions.

Dar El Qadi – the House of the Judge – was once the residence of a judge who had a zeal for astronomy. He was Muslim; the study of planets, stars, and galaxies, as well as of matter and energy in the universe at large, has long been important in the creed of Islam. Astronomy has been called the "queen of sciences". It is one of the oldest, embracing many subjects; physics and mathematics have a part to play in it. Numerous Muslim scientists and scholars have left their mark on the annals of astronomy. Some knowledge of it is thought be vital to an appreciation of the Islam religion.

The style of the house is an expression of Islamic culture. It has been restored faithfully to the time-honoured plans. Arched galleries surround the courtyard. Created in the image of paradise as it is written in the Qur'an, the garden has a fountain at its core. The house the judge built has an observatory tower that rises above the roof terrace, and looks over the souks and up to the stars above. You can have a taste of earthly bliss in such a setting. "Ye stars! which are the poetry of heaven ..." Lord Byron

Book to pack: "Scherezade goes West" by Fatima Mernissi

Dar El Qadi	
79, derb el Qadi	
Azbezt	
Marrakech Médina	
Morocco	
Tel: + 212 (24) 378 061	
Fax: + 212 (24) 384 596	
E-mail: darelqadi@hotmail.com	
Website: www.darelqadi.com	
www.great-escapes-hotels.com	

DIRECTIONS	Situated in the heart of the medina, it is located within a 5-minute walk from the main square of Marrakech, Djemaa el Fna
RATES	$$
ROOMS	6 and a hammam
FOOD	Traditional Moroccan dishes
HISTORY	An ancient house of a judge in the medina of Marrakech
X-FACTOR	Star-gazing at Arabian night skies from the terrace and the tower

Ein Zufluchtsort unter den Sternen

Wer die Konstellationen der Sterne kennt, wird nirgendwo
auf der Welt je verloren gehen. Sie sind wie himmlische
Wegweiser. Wer über die Sterne Bescheid weiß, weiß auch,
an welchem Breitengrad er sich befindet, wo Norden ist und
somit alle anderen Himmelsrichtungen.

Dar El Qadi – das Haus des Richters – war einst der Wohnsitz
eines Richters, der sich der Astronomie verschrieben hatte. Er
war Moslem und das Studium der Planeten, Sterne, Galaxien
sowie der Materie und Energie im All ist schon seit langer
Zeit ein wichtiger Bestandteil der Überzeugung des Islam.
Man nannte die Astronomie die Königin der Wissenschaften,
sie gehört zu den ältesten Wissenschaften und schließt viele
andere mit ein, darunter Mathematik und Physik. Zahlreiche
muslimische Wissenschaftler haben ihre Spuren in den
Annalen der Astronomie hinterlassen. Man sagt, dass ein
gewisses Wissen über dieses Fach unbedingt zur islamischen
Religion gehört.

Im Stil dieses Hauses spiegelt sich die islamische Kultur wider
und man hat es zeitgetreu restauriert. Gewölbte Galerien umgeben den Hof. Gemäß der Paradiesbeschreibung des Koran
befindet sich ein Springbrunnen im Zentrum des Gartens.
Das Haus, das der Richter einst erbaute, verfügt über einen
Beobachtungsturm, der sich über die Dachterrasse erhebt. Von
ihm aus überblickt man die Souks und den Sternenhimmel.
Solch ein Ort lässt einen ein wenig irdische Glückseligkeit
verspüren. »Ihr Sterne! Die Ihr die Poesie des Himmels
seid...« Lord Byron

Buchtipp: »Harem. Westliche Phantasien, östliche Wirklichkeit«
von Fatima Mernissi

Une retraite cosmique

Si vous connaissez les constellations et les étoiles, ces
« guides de la voûte céleste », vous retrouverez votre chemin
où que vous alliez. Si les étoiles vous sont familières, vous
saurez toujours à quelle latitude vous êtes : trouvez le nord
et vous trouverez toutes les autres directions.

Dar El Qadi, la Maison du Juge, fut autrefois la résidence
d'un juge féru d'astronomie, un musulman. Or, l'étude
des planètes, des astres, des galaxies, de la matière
et de l'énergie dans l'ensemble de l'univers est depuis
longtemps un aspect important de la croyance islamique.
L'astronomie, tenue pour la « reine des sciences », est l'une
des plus anciennes disciplines scientifiques. Elle englobe de
nombreux sujets, notamment la physique et les mathématiques.
Nombre de scientifiques et de savants musulmans ont marqué
de leur empreinte les annales de l'astronomie. La connaissance
de cette discipline est d'ailleurs considérée comme essentielle
à la compréhension de la religion islamique.

Le style de Dar El Qadi est l'expression de la culture islamique. Restaurée conformément à des plans d'époque, elle
présente une cour entourée de galeries cintrées. Son jardin,
élaboré à l'image du paradis décrit dans le Coran, accueille en
son centre une fontaine. La Maison du Juge dispose d'un
mirador qui se dresse au-dessus de la terrasse située sur le toit
et donne sur les *souks* et le ciel étoilé.
Un cadre merveilleux, fait pour goûter le bonheur ici-bas.
« La société a besoin de poètes, comme la nuit a besoin
d'étoiles ... » Lord Byron

Livre à emporter : « Le harem et l'occident » de Fatima Mernissi

ANREISE	Im Herzen der Medina gelegen, 5-minütiger Fußmarsch von Marrakeschs Hauptplatz, dem Djemaa el Fna entfernt
PREIS	$$
ZIMMER	6 und ein Hammam
KÜCHE	Traditionelle marokkanische Gerichte
GESCHICHTE	Das altehrwürdige Haus eines Richters in der Medina von Marrakesch
X-FAKTOR	Sternguckerei im arabischen Nachthimmel von der Terrasse und dem Turm aus

ACCÈS	Situé au cœur de la Médina, à 5 minutes à pied de Djemaa el Fna, la place principale de Marrakech
PRIX	$$
CHAMBRES	6, plus un hammam
RESTAURATION	Cuisine traditionnelle marocaine
HISTOIRE	Ancienne demeure d'un juge située dans la Médina de Marrakech
LES « PLUS »	Observation d'un ciel étoilé digne des Mille et Une Nuits depuis la terrasse et le mirador

Inner sanctum...
Riad Enija, Marrakech

Inner sanctum

It is usual to escape the bustle of the city by going to the country, to spend time in some quiet retreat. Here in the red-walled city of Marrakech you can have the best of both worlds in one place. Out of sight down a maze of narrow alleys in the medina is Riad Enija, once the town house – riad – of a silk trader. Now it is a small hotel, one that has been restored in a style faithful to its Islamic origin. Seclusion is key to the design.

Typically, riads have thick walls that insulate from the heat of the sun or the cold and most of the outside noise. Indoor and outdoor living space has always merged in the traditional Moroccan house. With an inner courtyard, the house centres on a walled garden. In the middle of the courtyard is a tiled fountain, often strewn with rose petals. It is a place of tranquillity for its residents, who are cloistered away from the outside world.

The colourful guesthouse is only a few minutes walk from the old city's huge main square, the Djemaa el Fna. From morning to night it teems with life. Orange and date sellers ply their trade; snake charmers, musicians, acrobats and storytellers amuse the crowds.

Book to pack: "Dreams of Trespass: Tales of a Harem Girlhood" by Fatima Mernissi

Riad Enija
Rahba Lakdima
9 Derb Mesfioui
Marrakech, Morocco
Tel: + 212 (24) 44 09 26/44 00 14
Fax: + 212 (24) 44 27 00
E-mail: riadenija@riadenija.com;
info@riadenija.com
Website: www.riadenija.com
www.great-escapes-hotels.com

DIRECTIONS	Only at a 5-minute walk from the Djemaa el Fna, Marrakech's central square
RATES	$$
ROOMS	4 rooms, 4 suites and 1 deluxe suite
FOOD	Good simple fare – light pastas, salads and grilled meats
HISTORY	Made up from two adjoining Riad houses, one being about 450 years old and the other 380 years old
X-FACTOR	Secret garden and charming authentic character

Im Innern Frieden

Normalerweise flieht man vor der hektischen Betriebsamkeit
der Stadt, indem man sich aufs Land zurückzieht, um etwas
Zeit in einem ruhigen Refugium zu verbringen. Hier, in der
rotwandigen Stadt Marrakesch kann man die Vorteile beider
Welten gleichzeitig genießen. Verborgen in einem Labyrinth
enger Gässchen, inmitten der Altstadt, liegt Riad Enija, einst
das Stadthaus – Riad – eines Seidenhändlers. Nun ist es ein
kleines Hotel – eines, das ganz im Stile seines islamischen
Ursprungs restauriert wurde. Abgeschiedenheit lautet dabei
das Geheimnis seiner Bauart.

Dicke Wände, die als Isolation gegen die Hitze der Sonne und
gegen Kälte dienen und den Großteil der Straßengeräusche
verschlucken, sind typisch für Riads. Immer schon sind Innen-
und Außenwohnräume in traditionellen Marokkanischen
Häusern miteinander verschmolzen. Im Zentrum des Hauses
liegt ein Innenhof mit einem von Mauern umrandeten Garten.
In dessen Mitte steht ein gekachelter Springbrunnen, oftmals
bestreut mit Rosenblüten. Für seine Bewohner, abgeschieden
von der Außenwelt, ist dies ein Ort der Ruhe.

Die farbenprächtige Unterkunft liegt nur wenige Gehminuten
vom großen Hauptplatz der Altstadt, dem Djemaa el Fna,
entfernt, wo von morgens bis abends das Leben pulsiert.
Orangen- und Dattelhändler betreiben ihr Gewerbe, Schlan-
genbeschwörer, Musikanten, Akrobaten und Geschichten-
erzähler unterhalten das Volk.

**Buchtipp: »Der Harem in uns. Die Furcht vor dem anderen
und die Sehnsucht der Frauen« von Fatima Mernissi**

Le saint des saints

On échappe généralement au tumulte et à l'agitation de la
ville en allant passer quelque temps à la campagne dans une
retraite paisible. Marrakech, la cité aux murs rouges, réunit
tous les avantages. Caché dans la médina, derrière un dédale
de ruelles étroites, se trouve Riad Enija. Cet ancien hôtel
particulier *(riad)* qui appartenait à un marchand de soie est
aujourd'hui un petit hôtel, restauré dans un style fidèle à ses
origines islamiques, avec une architecture qui préserve
l'intimité de ceux qui l'occupent.

Les riads ont généralement des murs épais qui les isolent
de la chaleur du soleil ou du froid et du bruit extérieur.
L'espace intérieur et l'espace extérieur ont toujours formé
un tout dans les maisons marocaines traditionnelles.
Le centre de l'hôtel Riad Enija est formé par une cour
intérieure et un jardin clos. Au milieu de cette cour se
trouve une fontaine carrelée, fréquemment parsemée de
pétales de rose. Dans ce lieu serein, les hôtes sont isolés
du monde extérieur.

Cette pension colorée se trouve à quelques minutes de
marche seulement de l'immense place principale de la
vieille ville, Djemaa el Fna, qui déborde de vie du matin au
soir avec ses vendeurs d'oranges et de dattes, ses charmeurs
de serpents, ses musiciens, ses acrobates et ses conteurs
qui amusent les badauds.

**Livre à emporter : « Rêves de femmes : Une enfance au harem »
de Fatima Mernissi**

ANREISE	Nur 5-minütiger Fußmarsch vom Djemaa el Fna, Marrakeschs Hauptplatz	ACCÈS	À 5 minutes à pied de Djemaa el Fna, la place centrale de Marrakech
PREIS	$$	PRIX	$$
ZIMMER	4 Zimmer, 4 Suiten und 1 Luxussuite	CHAMBRES	4 chambres, 4 suites et 1 suite de luxe
KÜCHE	Gute, einfache Kost – leichte Nudelgerichte, Salate und gegrilltes Fleisch	RESTAURATION	Cuisine simple et savoureuse : pâtes, salades et grillades
GESCHICHTE	Entstanden durch den Zusammenschluss zweier angrenzender Riads, von welchen eines etwa 450 Jahre alt ist, das andere 380 Jahre	HISTOIRE	L'hôtel est formé par la réunion de deux hôtels particuliers mitoyens dont l'un a environ 450 ans et l'autre 380 ans
X-FAKTOR	Geheimnisvoller Garten und bezaubernd authentischer Charakter	LES « PLUS »	Jardin secret et charme authentique

Five lantern luxury...

Riad El Mezouar, Marrakech

Riad El Mezouar, Marrakech

Five lantern luxury

Judgment has been passed on the merit of many places to stay. Worldwide, there are a variety of methods employed to indicate quality, from stars to numbers. Here in Morocco, some of the riads are rated on a scale of lanterns.

This seems rather an apt measure in a realm well known for its beautiful lamps. Decorative lanterns are widely used here; very much a part of the style that is Morocco. More often than not, they are what visitors take home with them. Riad El Mezouar has attained the top lantern rank; and it has a glow that is all of its own. From the bustling street outside, a door opens into a world where there is at once a sense of calm. This sudden feeling of peace is a planned effect. The pleasing symmetry of the columns and the garden are like an antidote to the disorder of life in the souk beyond the thick walls. At first sight, it may look simple: a courtyard with a large square-cut emerald pool, bounded on all sides by the classic galleries of this skilfully restored old house.

But there is inner decoration, done with a light yet sure hand. There are sumptuous touches here; rich velvet that is the colour of Moroccan merlot, old portraits, and filigree metal sconces that cast patterns of light on the wall. A covetous eye will look for their twins in the market. Such a lantern would be a radiant reminder of days and nights spent here.

Book to pack: "This Blinding Absence of Light" by Tahar Ben Jelloun

Riad El Mezouar	
28, Derb el Hammam, Issebtinne	
40000 Marrakech Medina	
Morocco	
Tel: + 212 (24) 38 09 49	
Fax: + 212 (24) 38 09 43	
E-mail: info@mezouar.com	
Website: www.mezouar.com	
www.great-escapes-hotels.com	

DIRECTIONS	A 10-minute walk from the Djemaa el Fna, Marrakech's central square
RATES	$$
ROOMS	3 suites, 2 double rooms
FOOD	Moroccan cuisine with French and Asian influences
HISTORY	The building dates from the eighteenth century
X-FACTOR	Hint of opulence, and the swimming pool

Fünf-Laternen-Luxus

Viele Hotels und Restaurants müssen Beurteilungen über sich ergehen lassen. Von Sternen bis zu Nummern – weltweit hat man verschiedene Methoden entwickelt, mit denen man diverse Qualitätsstandards zu bewerten versucht. In Marokko werden einige der Riads nach einer Skala von Laternen eingestuft, was in einer Gegend, die berühmt für ihre wundevollen Lampen ist, durchaus eine angebrachte Idee zu sein scheint. Überall werden hier dekorative Laternen benutzt. Sie gehören unabdingbar zum marokkanischen Stil, weshalb sie auch häufig von Besuchern als Souvenir mit nach Hause genommen werden. Mit seinem ihm eigenen Glühen hat Riad El Mezouar die Spitze der Laternenskala erreicht. Von dem Trubel der Straße aus öffnet sich eine Türe zu einer Welt, in der urplötzlich eine ruhige Stille herrscht. Dieses überraschende Gefühl des Friedens ist ein erwünschter und geplanter Effekt.

Die angenehme Symmetrie, die sich in der Anordnung der Säulen und des Gartens zeigt, wirkt wie ein Gegengift zu dem chaotischen Durcheinander, das jenseits dieser dicken Steinmauern auf dem Souk herrscht. Auf den ersten Blick mag hier alles sehr einfach erscheinen – ein Innenhof mit einem großen, eckigen, smaragdgrünen Becken, auf allen Seiten umrahmt von den klassischen Galerien dieses kunstvoll restaurierten alten Gebäudes.

Doch es gibt Verzierungen im Innenbereich, die auf einen dezenten, und dabei stilsicheren Geschmack schließen lassen. Samt in der Farbe von marokkanischem Merlot, alte Gemälde und filigrane, metallene Wandleuchter, die Lichtfiguren an die Wände werfen, lassen einen Hauch von Opulenz durch die Räume wehen. Und möglicherweise werden Ihre Augen begehrlich nach ähnlichen Gegenständen suchen, wenn Sie über die Märkte streifen. Eine solche Laterne könnte als strahlende Erinnerung an die hier verbrachten Tage und Nächte dienen.

Buchtipp: »Das Schweigen des Lichts« von Tahar Ben Jelloun

Cinq lanternes, la marque du luxe

Des jugements ont été portés sur la valeur de nombreuses destinations. Il existe dans le monde diverses méthodes visant à indiquer leur qualité, par exemple les étoiles ou les chiffres. Ici, au Maroc, certains riads sont classés à l'aide d'un système de lanternes.

Ce système d'évaluation semble tout à fait approprié dans un pays réputé pour la beauté de ses lampes. Les lanternes décoratives, très répandues ici, sont une partie intégrante du style marocain. Très souvent, ce sont ces lampes que les visiteurs ramènent de leur voyage.

Riad El Mezouar a obtenu le nombre maximum de lanternes et brille d'un éclat tout à fait particulier. De la rue débordante d'activité, une porte s'ouvre sur un univers où l'on éprouve immédiatement une impression de calme. Ce sentiment de quiétude soudain n'est pas dû au hasard : l'harmonieuse symétrie des colonnes et du jardin fait l'effet d'un antidote au désordre qui règne dans le souk, de l'autre côté des murs épais. À première vue, cette vieille maison habilement restaurée semble d'une grande simplicité : une cour avec un grand bassin carré couleur émeraude, bordée de tous côtés par des galeries classiques.

Toutefois, la décoration intérieure somptueuse, discrète mais réalisée de main de maître, contredit quelque peu cette impression : riches velours de la couleur du merlot marocain, vieux portraits et appliques métalliques en filigrane dessinant des motifs lumineux sur les murs. Ces dernières sont d'ailleurs si jolies qu'à n'en pas douter, les plus passionnés tenteront de dénicher leur réplique sur le marché. Des lanternes d'une beauté éclatante en souvenir des jours et des nuits passés ici.

Livre à emporter : « Cette aveuglante absence de lumière» de Tahar Ben Jelloun

ANREISE	20-minütiger Fußmarsch vom Djemaa el Fna, dem zentralen Platz in Marrakesch
PREIS	$$
ZIMMER	3 Suiten, 2 Doppelzimmer
KÜCHE	Lokale Restaurants oder auf Anfrage Abendessen im Hotel
GESCHICHTE	Das Gebäude stammt aus dem 19. Jahrhundert
X-FAKTOR	Ein Hauch von Opulenz und der Swimmingpool

ACCÈS	À 20 minutes à pied de Djemaa el Fna, la place centrale de Marrakech
PRIX	$$
CHAMBRES	3 suites, 2 chambres doubles
RESTAURATION	Possibilité de dîner à l'hôtel sur demande ou dans les restaurants alentour
HISTOIRE	Le bâtiment date du XIXe siècle
LES « PLUS »	Un soupçon d'opulence et la piscine

Deserted castle
Kasbah Aït Ben Moro, near Ouarzazate

Deserted castle

Slavery is still rife in this place; but don't make a fuss,
it's only in the movies.

For the 'dream weavers' of Hollywood, the desert sands
and vibrant cities of North Africa have long been preferred
locations. It is in part the quality of the light, dry, clear and
bright, that draws filmmakers. Additionally, the stunning
landscape of great sand dunes, lush, palm-filled oases, and
snow-capped mountains helps create a whole range of film
backdrops, from the epic "Lawrence of Arabia" to
"Gladiator".

Kasbah Ben Moro is no film set. It is an authentic old castle,
now acting in a new role; being a hotel. Built in the 17th
Century, it gives guests a feel of old Morocco. The stylish yet
simple rooms are on all three levels of the Kasbah's towers.
Scenes of the High Atlas Mountains, and the ruins of the
old Amerhidil Kasbah are spread out below; the rich green
palm grove in this stark desert landscape is quite a theatrical
contrast. The kasbah is in the quiet little village of Skoura.
At night, it is very still, and the stars shine bright above.

It is not far from here to the much busier resort town of
Ouarzazate, which is the focus of the Moroccan film in-
dustry. You can tour the sets built for "Asterix & Obelix 2",
Timothy Dalton's "Cleopatra" and "Kundun", and more.
Some of the guides will tell you they have been slaves, but
it was only on screen.

**Book to pack: "A Life Full of Holes" by Driss Ben Hamed
Charhadi**

Kasbah Aït Ben Moro		
Skoura		
Morocco	DIRECTIONS	30 minutes south of Ouarzazate; four and a half hours drive southeast from Marrakech
Tel: + 212 (24) 85 21 16	RATES	$
Fax: + 212 (24) 85 20 16	ROOMS	13 double rooms
E-mail: hotelbenmoro@yahoo.fr	FOOD	Simple but good
Website: www.passionmaroc.com	HISTORY	17th Century fort, restored and recently converted to a hotel
www.great-escapes-hotels.com	X-FACTOR	Dramatic landscape, with fields of roses

Ein Palast in der Wüste

Hier ist die Sklaverei noch weit verbreitet, doch keine Aufregung, – natürlich nur in Filmen. Seit langem schon gehören der Wüstensand und die pulsierenden Städte Nordafrikas zu den beliebtesten Drehorten von Hollywoods Traumfabrikanten. Was die Filmemacher hierher zieht, ist zum Teil die Lichtqualität, trocken, klar und hell. Außerdem kann die überwältigende Landschaft aus großen Sanddünen, grünen Palmenoasen und schneebedeckten Berggipfeln als Kulisse für die verschiedensten Filme dienen, vom Epos »Lawrence von Arabien«, bis hin zu »Gladiator«.
Kasbah Ben Moro ist kein Drehort, sondern ein authentischer alter Palast, der nun in eine neue Rolle als Hotel geschlüpft ist. Im 17. Jahrhundert erbaut, vermittelt er den Gästen ein Gefühl für das Marokko der alten Zeit. Die stilvollen, doch einfachen Räume befinden sich auf allen drei Etagen des Turms der Kashbah. Darunter erstreckt sich das Panorama über das hohe Atlasgebirge und die Ruinen der alten Kashbah Amerhidil. Der dichte, grüne Palmenhain bildet einen geradezu theatralischen Kontrastpunkt in dieser vollkommenen Wüstenlandschaft. Die Kashbah befindet sich in dem kleinen, ruhigen Dorf Skoura, wo des Nachts eine vollkommene Stille herrscht und die Sterne hell am Himmel glitzern.
Von hier aus ist es nicht mehr weit nach Ouarzazate, einem Urlaubsort, in dem weitaus mehr Trubel herrscht; es ist die Hauptstadt der marokkanischen Filmindustrie. Hier können Sie die Drehorte von »Asterix und Obelix 2«, Timothy Daltons »Kleopatra«, sowie »Kundun« und einige andere besuchen. Manche Führer werden Ihnen erklären, dass sie Sklaven waren, aber nur auf der Leinwand.
Buchtipp: »Ein Leben voller Fallgruben« von Driss Ben Hamed Charhadi

La forteresse des sables

Ici, l'esclavage reste chose commune, mais rassurez-vous, uniquement dans les films.
Les sables du désert et les villes hautes en couleur d'Afrique du Nord font partie depuis longtemps des lieux de tournage favoris des « faiseurs de rêve » d'Hollywood. C'est notamment la qualité de la lumière, nette, pure et éclatante, qui attire les cinéastes. Par ailleurs, le superbe paysage d'immenses dunes de sable, de montagnes enneigées et d'oasis luxuriantes où poussent de nombreux palmiers a servi et sert encore aujourd'hui de toile de fond à toutes sortes de longs-métrages, de « Lawrence d'Arabie » à « Gladiator ».
La Kasbah Ben Moro n'est pas un décor de cinéma. Il s'agit d'un vieux château authentique qui interprète aujourd'hui un nouveau rôle, celui d'un hôtel. Construit au XVIIe siècle, il permet aux hôtes de retrouver l'atmosphère du Maroc d'autrefois. Les chambres au style étudié mais simple sont réparties sur les trois niveaux des tours de la casbah. Vous verrez en contrebas le Haut Atlas et les ruines de l'ancienne casbah d'Amerhidil. Le contraste entre la désolation du paysage désertique et la luxuriance de la palmeraie verdoyante est assez spectaculaire. La casbah se trouve dans le petit village de Skoura. La nuit, une grande tranquillité y règne et les étoiles brillent dans le ciel.
La Kasbah Ben Moro est situé à proximité d'Ouarzazate, ville touristique beaucoup plus animée et centre de l'industrie cinématographique du pays. Vous pourrez visiter les décors construits pour le tournage d' « Astérix & Obélix 2 », de « Cléopâtre » par Timothy Dalton, de « Kundun », etc. Certains guides vous diront qu'ils ont un jour été esclaves, mais seulement le temps d'un film.
Livre à emporter : « Une vie pleine de trous » de Driss Ben Hamed Charhadi

ANREISE	30 Minuten südlich von Ouarzazate; viereinhalb-stündige Fahrt südöstlich von Marrakesch
PREIS	$
ZIMMER	13 Doppelzimmer
KÜCHE	Einfach aber gut
GESCHICHTE	Burg aus dem 17. Jahrhundert, kürzlich renoviert und zum Hotel umgebaut
X-FAKTOR	Spektakuläre Landschaft mit Rosenfeldern

ACCÈS	À 30 minutes d'Ouarzazate par le sud et à 4H30 en voiture de Marrakech par le sud-est
PRIX	$
CHAMBRES	13 chambres doubles
RESTAURATION	Simple mais savoureuse
HISTOIRE	Fort datant du XVIIe siècle, restauré et récemment transformé en hôtel
LES « PLUS »	Paysage spectaculaire où l'on peut admirer des champs de roses

Open Sesame...
Hotel Dar Cherait, Tozeur

Hotel Dar Cherait, Tozeur

Open Sesame

You can experience some of the magic of the Arabian Nights here, in much less than one thousand and one nights.

On the edge of the Sahara, in the town of Tozeur, there is a whole park themed on that fabulous fable. But you don't need the magic words said by Ali Baba to open the doors of this plush palace. A credit card is the usual "Open Sesame" in the real world.

The opulence of the Hotel Dar Cherait is in line with the fairy tale, even though it has been furnished with 'leftovers'. The Cherait family first built a museum – the one that is nearby – to house their large collection of Tunisian artefacts. Then they built the hotel; so all the furniture, paintings, and pieces that could not be fitted into the museum were put on display there. Ornate carpets and dazzling tiles enhance the rich Moorish style.

Dar Cherait is in the heart of a great grove of palm trees, thanks to an Arab mathematician who first worked out the best way to bring water to a garden parched by fierce sun. Ibn Shabbat devised a complex system of irrigation channels – one that still winds all through the town. That was back in the 13th century; Tozeur owes its lushness now to his skill then. Thousands upon thousands of palm trees have been able to grow here in the oasis he started, and in many others like it.

Book to pack: "Arabian Nights and Days" by Naguib Mahfouz

Hotel Dar Cherait
Route Touristique de Tozeur Tunisia
2200 Tozeur
Tunisia
Tel: + 216 (76) 4521 00
Fax: + 216 (76) 4523 29
E-mail: darcherait@planet.tn
Website: www.darcherait.com.tn
www.great-escapes-hotels.com

DIRECTIONS	500 km/310 m south of Tunis; 5 minutes from the Airport Tozeur/Nefta
RATES	$$
ROOMS	73 double rooms, 12 suites
FOOD	Tunisian and Western style menu, famous for its dates
HISTORY	Opened in 1995
X-FACTOR	The marvellous natural landscape around the oasis, and the magnificent brickwork of the architecture

Sesam, öffne Dich

Hier können Sie den Zauber arabischer Nächte erleben, und zwar in weniger als tausend und einer Nacht. Am Rande der Sahara, in der Stadt Tozeur, liegt ein ganzer Park, in dem sich alles um diese berühmten Erzählungen dreht. Die magischen Worte, die Ali Baba einst aussprach, benötigen Sie nicht, um sich Zutritt zu diesem vornehmen Palast zu verschaffen. In der wirklichen Welt dient eine Kreditkarte als »Sesam, öffne Dich«.

In seiner prachtvollen Ausstattung kann das Hotel Dar Cherait leicht mit dem Märchen mithalten, obwohl es mit »Überbleibseln« eingerichtet wurde. Die Familie Cherait hatte nämlich zunächst ein Museum gebaut – es liegt ganz in der Nähe – um dort ihre umfangreiche Sammlung tunesischer Kunstwerke zu zeigen. Anschließend errichteten sie das Hotel und alle Möbel, Gemälde und Kunstgegenstände, die in dem Museum keinen Platz mehr fanden, wurden hier zur Schau gestellt. Reich verzierte Teppiche und bunte Kacheln tragen zu dem üppigen, maurischen Stil bei.

Dass Dar Cherait im Herzen eines großen Palmenhaines liegt, verdankt es einem arabischen Mathematiker, der erstmals eine geeignete Methode entwickelte, mit der die von der glühenden Sonne ausgetrockneten Gärten bewässert werden konnte. Ibn Shabbat entwickelte ein komplexes System von Bewässerungskanälen, das die gesamte Stadt durchzieht. All dies geschah im 13. Jahrhundert; immer noch verdankt Tozeur heute sein saftiges Grün den außergewöhnlichen Fähigkeiten dieses Mannes. Tausende und Abertausende von Palmen konnten seitdem in der Oase, die er einst begründete, sowie in vielen ähnlichen anderen, wachsen.

Buchtipp: »Die Nacht der Tausend Nächte« von Naguib Mahfouz

Sésame, ouvre-toi

Cet endroit vous permettra de connaître un peu la magie des Mille et Une Nuits, à ceci près que votre séjour ne durera pas aussi longtemps. Dans la ville de Tozeur, située en bordure du Sahara, se trouve un parc entièrement consacré à cette fable extraordinaire. Nul besoin de prononcer la formule magique d'Ali Baba pour se faire ouvrir les portes de ce somptueux palace. Dans le monde réel, c'est la carte de crédit qui fait office de « Sésame, ouvre-toi ».

Bien que l'hôtel Dar Cherait ait été meublé avec des « restes », son luxe est à la hauteur de celui décrit dans le conte. Avant de l'édifier, la famille Cherait fit construire un musée (aujourd'hui voisin de l'hôtel) afin d'y abriter sa vaste collection d'objets d'art tunisiens. Dar Cherait a donc hérité de tous les meubles, peintures et objets qui, faute de place, ne pouvaient pas être exposés dans le musée. Des tapis richement ornés et des carreaux de faïence d'une beauté éblouissante mettent en valeur le splendide style maure de l'hôtel.

L'hôtel est installé au cœur d'une superbe palmeraie qui n'existerait pas sans un mathématicien arabe, Ibn Shabbat, inventeur d'une solution judicieuse pour amener l'eau jusqu'à un jardin desséché par un soleil implacable. Ce savant mit au point un système complexe de canaux d'irrigation que l'on peut encore aujourd'hui voir serpenter dans toute la ville. Cette invention date du XIIIe siècle, et Tozeur doit sa luxuriance actuelle à ce savoir-faire du passé. La technique de Shabbat a en effet permis à des dizaines de milliers de palmiers de pousser dans l'oasis qu'il fit naître, et dans bien d'autres semblables.

Livre à emporter : « Les mille et une nuits » de Naguib Mahfouz

ANREISE	500 km südlich von Tunis, 5 Minuten vom Flughafen Tozeur/Nefta entfernt
PREIS	$$
ZIMMER	73 Doppelzimmer, 12 Suiten
KÜCHE	Tunesische und westliche Gerichte, berühmt für seine Datteln
GESCHICHTE	Eröffnet im Jahr 1995
X-FAKTOR	Die märchenhaft schöne natürliche Landschaft, welche die Oase umgibt, und die großartige Ziegelarchitektur

ACCÈS	À 500 km au sud de Tunis, à 5 minutes de l'aéroport Tozeur/Nefta.
PRIX	$$
CHAMBRES	73 chambres doubles, 12 suites
RESTAURATION	Cuisine tunisienne et occidentale, célèbre pour ses plats à base de dattes
HISTOIRE	Ouvert en 1995
LES « PLUS »	Magnifique paysage autour de l'oasis et superbe architecture à base de briquetage

In a sea of sand...

Adrere Amellal Desert Eco-Lodge, Siwa Oasis

Adrere Amellal Desert Eco-Lodge, Siwa Oasis

In a sea of sand

Deep in Egypt's Western desert there is an oasis within an oasis. Nestled at the foot of the wind-sculpted White Mountain from which it takes its name, Adrere Amellal Lodge is built from palm beams, salt rock and clay, a local construction technique known as kershaf. The buildings are almost invisible in the landscape, their pale colour blending into the sand.

Set in acres of desert on the edge of Siwa Lake, the simple yet luxurious eco-lodge has its own date and olive orchard; a stunning swimming pool is formed around an old Roman spring. So that no electricity obscures the moon and stars, handmade candles provide the lighting, and on cold winter nights, coal-filled braziers warm the air. On the other side of the lake the great Sand Sea, one of the world's largest dune fields, undulates towards the horizon.

Ancient tombs and temples close by are testament to Siwa's long and illustrious history. It was here to the Temple of the Oracle that the Greek warrior Alexander the Great came, in 331 B.C. He sought confirmation that he was a god, more than the extraordinary man he was.

In this remote and beautiful location there is the chance for mere mortals to travel through one of the least explored deserts on earth.

Book to pack: "The Alexandria Quartet" by Lawrence Durrell

Adrere Amellal Desert Eco-Lodge
Siwa Oasis
18 Mansour Mohamed Street
Zamalek 11211, Cairo
Egypt
Tel: + 20 (2) 736 78 79
Fax: + 20 (2) 735 54 89
E-mail: info@eqi.com.eg
Website: www.andrereamellal.net
www.great-escapes-hotels.com

DIRECTIONS	Currently an 8-10 hour journey by air-conditioned jeep west from Cairo or Alexandria, air access planned
RATES	$$$
ROOMS	27 double rooms
FOOD	Egyptian and European cuisine for gourmets, most food organically grown in the lodge garden
HISTORY	Egypt's first eco-lodge, opened in 1997
X-FACTOR	"English Patient" territory

In einem Meer aus Sand

Tief im Innern der westlichen Wüste Ägyptens liegt eine
Oase in einer Oase. Die Adrere Amellal Lodge, ein Bauwerk
aus Palmstämmen, Salzgestein und Lehm – eine für diese
Gegend typische Bautechnik, die auch als Kershaf bezeich-
net wird – schmiegt sich an den Fuß des windgegerbten
White Mountain, von dem die Lodge auch ihren Namen hat.
Da ihre helle Farbe der des Sandes gleicht, sind ihre
Gebäude in der Landschaft beinahe nicht auszumachen.
Die einfache und gleichzeitig luxuriöse »Öko-Lodge«, die
inmitten eines riesigen Wüstengebietes am Rande des
Siwa Sees liegt, hat ihren eigenen Dattel- und Olivengarten
und ein großartiges Schwimmbecken wurde um eine alte
römische Quelle gebaut. Damit kein elektrisches Licht die
Mond- und Sternennächte erhellt, sorgen ausschließlich
handgemachte Kerzen für Beleuchtung und an kalten
Winterabenden erwärmen glühende Kohlebecken die
Luft. Auf der anderen Seite des Sees wellt sich das große
Sandmeer, eine der größten Dünenlandschaften der Erde,
dem Horizont entgegen.
Nahegelegene alte Grabstätten und Tempel zeugen von
Siwas langer und glänzender Geschichte. Im Jahre 331 v.
Chr. geschah es, dass der griechische Feldherr Alexander der
Große hierher zum Orakeltempel kam um sich bestätigen
zu lassen, dass er nicht nur ein außergewöhnlicher Mann,
sondern gar ein Gott sei. Dieser abgeschiedene und schöne
Ort bietet Normalsterblichen die Gelegenheit durch eine der
am wenigsten erforschten Wüsten der Welt zu reisen.
Buchtipp: »Das Alexandria-Quartett« von Lawrence Durrell

Dans une mer de sable

Il existe, au cœur du désert occidental égyptien, une oasis au
milieu d'une oasis. Niché au pied de la Montagne Blanche
sculptée par le vent dont il tire son nom, Adrere Amellal
Lodge a été érigé à partir de madriers de palmier, de roche
saline et d'argile salifère, selon une technique de construction locale appelée *kershaf*. Les bâtiments sont ainsi presque
invisibles, leur nuance pâle se fondant dans le sable.
Situé au centre d'un immense désert, au bord du lac Siouah,
cet hôtel écologique simple mais luxueux dispose d'un ver-
ger de dattes et d'olives mais également d'une superbe piscine construite autour d'une ancienne source romaine. Afin
que l'électricité ne fasse pas d'ombre à la lune et aux étoiles,
des bougies faites à la main sont utilisées en guise d'éclairage et, durant les froides nuits d'hiver, des braseros réchauf-
fent l'atmosphère. De l'autre côté du lac, l'immense mer de
sable, l'un des champs de dunes les plus grands du monde,
s'étend en ondulations jusqu'à l'horizon.
Les tombeaux et les temples antiques voisins témoignent de
la longue et glorieuse histoire de Siouah : c'est ici, dans le
Temple de l'oracle, que le guerrier grec Alexandre le Grand
vint chercher confirmation en 331 av. J.-C. qu'il était non pas
un homme extraordinaire hors du commun mais bien un
dieu. Ce site isolé et majestueux est l'occasion pour les
simples mortels de découvrir l'un des déserts les moins
explorés de la planète.
**Livre à emporter : « Le quatuor d'Alexandrie » de Lawrence
Durrell**

ANREISE	Momentan 8-10-stündige Fahrt in einem klimatisiertem Jeep westlich von Kairo oder Alexandria aus, eine Flug-verbindung ist geplant
PREIS	$$$
ZIMMER	27 Doppelzimmer
KÜCHE	Ägyptische und europäische Küche für Feinschmecker; ein Großteil des Gemüses stammt aus biologischem Anbau aus dem hauseigenen Garten
GESCHICHTE	Ägyptens erste Öko-Lodge, eröffnet im Jahre 1997
X-FAKTOR	Landschaft wie in »Der englische Patient«

ACCÈS	À 8-10 heures à l'ouest du Caire ou d'Alexandrie en jeep climatisée. L'accès par avion est en projet
PRIX	$$$
CHAMBRES	27 chambres doubles
RESTAURATION	Cuisine gastronomique égyptienne et européenne. La plupart des produits sont cultivés biologiquement dans le jardin de l'hôtel
HISTOIRE	Ouvert en 1997, il s'agit du premier hôtel écologique de l'Égypte
LES « PLUS »	Cadre du « Patient anglais »

A painterly retreat.
Hotel Marsam, Luxor West Bank

A painterly retreat

This is the place where the nobility of the country stayed. Well, if the truth must be told, not exactly right here, but very close – and they never left. 'They' are the long dead. Preserved forever, people come here to see them in their tombs.

The ancient village of Qurna, on the west bank of the Nile at Luxor, is perched on hills, rock honeycombed with tombs. It's here in the midst of this great open-air museum that the Hotel Marsam stands. It's no wonder then that it is one of the most preferred 'digs' of archaeologists. This is the closest you can get to being in ruins, and by choice. Artists come here too, for the wealth of subjects. In fact, the word Marsam is Arabic for "a painter's studio." From 1941, graduate fine art students lived in part of the hotel. For the next three decades, it was like Montmartre in Paris. The art students are long gone but the hotel art gallery installed next door carries on the tradition.

The simple mud brick building sits alongside waving date palms and fields of sugar cane. It is typical of the adobe style once common but now rare in Nubia and Upper Egypt. Most of the life of the hotel is centred in the lush garden. It opens to the east with a view over the fields towards the Nile and the Colossi of Memnon. The twin statues are almost all that is left of the once vast mortuary temple of Amenhotep III.

Book to pack: "An Egyptian Journal" by William Golding

Hotel Marsam
Qurna
Luxor West Bank
Egypt
Tel: + 20 (95) 237 24 03
E-mail: marsam@africamail.com
Website: www.luxor-westbank.com
www.great-escapes-hotels.com

DIRECTIONS	Beside the Ticket Office, Luxor West Bank
RATES	$
ROOMS	4 renovated rooms, 20 standard rooms
FOOD	Popular Egyptian and European dishes; authentic "solar" bread served with every meal
HISTORY	Some of the buildings of the hotel were built in 1920 to house archaeologists. The rest were built between 1940 and 1970 by Ali Abdul Rasoul, who was the owner of the hotel at that time
X-FACTOR	Simple living in the dead centre of history

Ein malerisches Versteck

Hier ist es, wo die Adeligen des Landes verweilten. Um exakt zu sein, nicht genau hier, aber ganz in der Nähe – und sie haben diesen Ort niemals verlassen. »Sie« sind seit langer Zeit tot. Menschen kommen hierher, um sie in ihren Gräbern zu sehen, wo sie, für die Ewigkeit konserviert, liegen. Das antike Dorf Qurna liegt auf Hügeln am westlichen Nil-ufer in Luxor – Felsgestein, bienenwabenartig mit Gräbern gespickt. Hier, in der Mitte dieses großartigen Freilichtmu-seums, steht das Hotel Marsam. Dass dies eine der begehrtes-ten Ausgrabungsstätten für Archäologen ist, überrascht daher kaum. Nirgendwo sonst kann man so nah an Ruinen (nicht am Ruin) sein, wie hier. Auch Künstler kommen hier-her, wegen der Fülle an Motiven. Der Begriff Marsam steht im Arabischen für »Malerwerkstatt«. Ab 1941 lebten Studien-absolventen der bildenden Künste in einem Teil dieses Hotels. Für die darauffolgenden drei Jahrzehnte war es das, was Mont-martre für Paris ist. Zwar sind die Kunststudenten längst ver-schwunden, doch in der hoteleigenen Kunstgalerie, die gleich nebenan eingerichtet wurde, besteht diese Tradition fort. Das einfache Schlamm- und Ziegelgebäude grenzt an wogende Dattelpalmen und Zuckerrohrfelder an und entspricht ganz dem Stil der luftgetrockneten Lehmhäuser, die in Nubien und Oberägypten einst weit verbreitet waren, nun aber sehr selten geworden sind. Das Hotelleben spielt sich hauptsächlich in dem sattgrünen Garten ab. Nach Osten hin eröffnet sich von hier der Blick über die Felder in Richtung Nil und den Mem-non-Koloss. Die Zwillingsstatuen sind beinahe das Einzige, was von dem einst mächtigen Grabtempel Amenhoteps II noch übrig ist.

Buchtipp: »Ein ägyptisches Tagebuch. Reisen, um glücklich zu sein« von William Golding

Le refuge des peintres

C'est ici, ou pour être exact, tout près d'ici, que résidaient les nobles du pays. Et ils n'en sont jamais partis. Disparus depuis longtemps, préservés pour l'éternité, c'est à leurs tombeaux que l'on rend aujourd'hui visite.

Le village antique de Qurna, sur la rive ouest du Nil, à Louxor, est perché sur des collines truffées de tombeaux. C'est au cœur de cet immense musée en plein air que se dresse l'hôtel Marsam. Alentour, tout n'est que ruine, par choix. Rien d'étonnant à ce que ce site soit l'un des lieux de fouille préférés des archéologues. Les artistes y viennent également en nombre, attirés par la richesse des sujets à disposition. De fait, « Marsam » signifie « atelier de peintre » en arabe. En 1941, les étudiants diplômés des Beaux-Arts commencèrent à venir s'installer dans une partie de l'hôtel, et pendant les trois décennies suivantes, l'endroit ressem-blait à Montmartre. Les étudiants en art sont partis depuis longtemps, mais la galerie d'art de l'hôtel, qui jouxte celui-ci, perpétue la tradition.

L'édifice simple, construit avec des briques d'argile séchées au soleil, côtoie des dattiers et des champs de canne à sucre qui se balancent sous le vent. Ces constructions en adobe, autrefois courantes en Nubie et en Haute Égypte, y sont rares de nos jours. La plus grande partie de l'activité de l'hôtel a lieu dans son jardin luxuriant. Celui-ci s'ouvre vers l'est et offre une vue sur un paysage de champs puis, à l'horizon, sur le Nil et les Colosses de Memnon. Ces deux statues jumelles sont les uniques vestiges du vaste temple funéraire d'Amhénotep III.

Livre à emporter : « Journal égyptien » de William Golding

ANREISE	Neben dem Ticketschalter, in Luxor West Bank
PREIS	$
ZIMMER	4 renovierte Räume, 20 Standardzimmer
KÜCHE	Bekannte ägyptische und europäische Gerichte; zu jedem Essen wird echtes »Sonnenbrot« gereicht
GESCHICHTE	Einige Teile des Hotels wurden 1920 für die Unterbrin-gung von Archäologen gebaut. Die übrigen errichtete Ali Abdul Rasoul, der damalige Hotelbesitzer, zwischen 1940 und 1970
X-FAKTOR	Einfach leben, im Totenzentrum der Geschichte

ACCÈS	À côté du bureau de vente de billets, rive ouest du Nil
PRIX	$
CHAMBRES	4 chambres rénovées, 20 chambres standard
RESTAURATION	Cuisine populaire égyptienne et européenne. Chaque repas est accompagné d'authentique pain « solaire »
HISTOIRE	Certains bâtiments de l'hôtel datent des années 20. Ils étaient destinés à accueillir les archéologues. Le reste a été construit entre les années 40 et les années 70 par Ali Abdul Rasoul, propriétaire de l'hôtel à l'époque
LES « PLUS »	Vie simple au centre funéraire de l'Histoire

A palace fit for Cleopatra...
Hotel Al Moudira, Luxor

A palace fit for Cleopatra

Do you fancy the life of a pharaoh? Or to live like a queen,
such as the lovely Cleopatra?

Of course you are too late; those dynasties are long in their
tombs, but you can be a slave to luxury staying here in this
modern temple. You will be given the royal treatment in a
setting that is duly lavish.

Al Moudira Hotel has just risen up on the West bank of
the Nile, where the most splendid ancient sites are to be
found. This latter-day palace is no more than a few minutes
away from the Valley of the Kings. It was there that the
most famous of the pharaohs – Seti I, Ramses II, and
Tutankhamen – were laid to rest. Until they were dug up,
that is, and all their grandeur revealed – then plundered.
The hotel has been built on the edge of where fields end
and the desert begins. Sugar cane growers tend their land
just as their ancestors have done for thousands of years.
In contrast to this simplicity, as has always been the custom,
there is this grand hotel, a work of art in a realm full of
them. Its walls enclose a lush garden; the air is fragrant
with jasmine and henna. Maybe these photographs might
serve you and me both as a modern kind of hieroglyphics;
those ancient images that showed the viewer how others
lived once they could, at last, be read.

So, as I am in charge, I will let this 'dazzling mosaic' of
images tell their own tale.

Book to pack: "Antony and Cleopatra" by William Shakespeare

Hotel Al Moudira		
Luxor		
Egypt		
Tel: + 20 (12) 325 13 07		
Fax: + 20 (12) 322 05 28		
E-mail: contact@moudira.com		
Website: www.moudira.com		
www.great-escapes-hotels.com		

DIRECTIONS	20 minutes from Luxor airport	
RATES	$$	
ROOMS	54	
FOOD	Mediterranean inspired, with Levantine and oriental flavours	
HISTORY	Opened in 2002, designed by owner Zeina Aboukheir together with architect Olivier Sednaoui, and integrating pieces saved from old Egyptian buildings	
X-FACTOR	Living like Cleopatra now	

Ein Palast wie für Cleopatra

Würden Sie gerne leben wie ein Pharao? Oder wie eine Königin, beispielsweise die bezaubernde Cleopatra? Dafür sind Sie freilich zu spät dran, längst ruhen diese Dynastien in ihren Gräbern. Aber wenn Sie sich für einen Aufenthalt in diesem modernen Tempel entscheiden sollten, können Sie einem Luxus frönen, der dem ihren gleichkommt. In einer entsprechend prachtvollen Umgebung können Sie sich wahrhaft königlich verwöhnen lassen. Das Al Moudira Hotel wurde erst kürzlich am westlichen Nilufer errichtet, also dort, wo sich der größte Teil der großartigen alten Sehenswürdigkeiten befindet. Dieser neuzeitliche Palast liegt nur einige Minuten vom Tal der Könige entfernt. Hier wurden Seti I, Ramses II, sowie Tutenchamun in ihre letzte Ruhestätte gelegt – zumindest bis man sie wieder ausgrub, das Geheimnis ihrer ganzen Größe aufdeckte und ihre Gräber schließlich ausplünderte.

Das Hotel wurde dort errichtet, wo bewirtschaftete Felder und Wüste ineinander übergehen. Zuckerrohrbauern bestellen ihre Felder noch genauso, wie es ihre Vorfahren seit Tausenden von Jahren getan haben. Dieses Grand Hotel steht in unmittelbarem Gegensatz zu einer solchen Einfachheit. Ein Kontrast, wie er hier immer üblich war. Es ist ein Kunstwerk in einem Königreich voll Kunstwerken. Seine Mauern umschließen einen üppigen Garten und die Luft duftet nach Jasmin und Henna. Vielleicht können diese Abbildungen Ihnen ja als eine Art moderner Hieroglyphen dienen, jene altertümlichen Bilder, die dem Betrachter Aufschluss über die Lebensweise vergangener Kulturen gaben, als man sie schließlich entziffern konnte. Da es nun an mir ist, Ihnen einen Eindruck zu vermitteln, werde ich einfach dieses wundervolle Mosaik von Bildern für sich selbst sprechen lassen.

Buchtipp: »Antonius und Cleopatra« von William Shakespeare

Un palais pour Cléopâtre

Vous rêvez de vivre la vie d'un pharaon ? Ou la vie d'une reine, peut-être, par exemple celle de la délicieuse Cléopâtre ? Bien sûr, vous arrivez un peu tard. Ces dynasties sont depuis bien longtemps enfouies dans la tombe. Cependant, Al Moudira vous donne aujourd'hui la possibilité de faire un séjour dans le luxe d'un temple moderne et d'être traité comme un roi dans un cadre forcément fastueux.

De construction récente, l'hôtel Al Moudira s'élève sur la rive ouest du Nil, où se trouvent les plus beaux sites antiques. Ce palace des temps modernes n'est qu'à quelques minutes de la Vallée des Rois où reposaient les pharaons les plus célèbres, Séti Ier, Ramsès II et Toutankhamon, jusqu'à l'exhumation et le pillage de leurs sarcophages qui révélèrent leur magnificence.

L'hôtel est situé à la limite entre les champs et le désert. Les cultivateurs de canne à sucre travaillent la terre de la même manière que leurs ancêtres depuis des milliers d'années. Cette simplicité, habituelle ici, contraste avec ce grand hôtel, véritable œuvre d'art dans une contrée où on ne compte plus les merveilles. Ses murs renferment un jardin luxuriant, où jasmins et hennés embaument l'air. Nous pouvons peut-être utiliser ces photos comme un genre nouveau de hiéroglyphes, ces dessins antiques qui, une fois déchiffrés, révélèrent le mode de vie d'une autre civilisation.

Laissons donc cette extraordinaire mosaïque d'images parler d'elle-même.

Livre à emporter : « Antoine et Cléopâtre » de William Shakespeare

ANREISE	20 Minuten vom Flughafen Luxor
PREIS	$$
ZIMMER	54
KÜCHE	Mediterran mit levantinischen und orientalischen Geschmäckern
GESCHICHTE	Entworfen vom Besitzer Zeina Aboukheir und dem Architekten Olivier Sednaoui, wurde das Hotel im Jahr 2002 eröffnet; Bauteile die aus alten ägyptischen Gebäuden stammen und erhalten werden konnten, wurden dabei integriert
X-FAKTOR	In unserer Zeit wie Cleopatra leben

ACCÈS	À 20 minutes de l'aéroport de Louxor
PRIX	$$
CHAMBRES	54
RESTAURATION	D'inspiration méditerranéenne. Saveurs levantines et orientales
HISTOIRE	Ouvert en 2002, conçu par le propriétaire, Zeina Aboukheir, en collaboration avec l'architecte Olivier Sednaoui, cet hôtel réunit des objets provenant dans d'anciennes constructions égyptiennes
LES « PLUS »	Vivre comme Cléopâtre à notre époque

Time travel on the Nile...

M.S. Kasr Ibrim & M.S. Eugenie, Lake Nasser

M.S. Kasr Ibrim & M.S. Eugenie, Lake Nasser

Time travel on the Nile

In Egyptian belief, and in daily life, boats have played a dual part, being borth a means of transport and a symbol of hope. The sun god Ra was thought to travel across the sky in a solar ship; and it was held that those who were worthy might join Osiris, the god of the dead, in his divine bark after death. That would be the infinite cruise.

But why wait for the next world? You can take this trip now. Aboard the M.S. Kasr Ibrim and M.S. Eugenie, you can bridge the age of the Pharaohs and the Flappers. The great monuments of the former are before you on the banks of the Nile; these splendid steamers on Lake Nasser call to mind the latter, with their Art Deco style.

One boat is named after the citadel of Kasr Ibrim, a relic of Nubia, the 'land of gold', one of ancient Egypt's richest states. The once mighty fortress has stood here for aeons; other temples were moved here, to higher ground, when the Aswan Dam was built. Sailing here, you will see what is left of a once fabulous past. The journey takes you from wonders such as the Avenue of the Sphinxes to the grand finale, the Great Temples of Ramses II at Abu Simbel. Time and nature may have worn down their glory, but they are still amazing to see.

On board the glamour has not faded. There is grandness on a scale that suits the location it sails in. What better way to see the splendour of Egypt than from the decks of these deluxe ships?

Book to pack: "Death on the Nile" by Agatha Christie

M.S. Kasr Ibrim & M.S. Eugenie
Lake Nasser
Nubia
Egypt
Tel: + 20 (2) 516 9653
Fax: + 20 (2) 516 9646
E-mail: eugenie@eugenie.com.eg
Website: www.kasribrim.com.eg
www.great-escapes-hotels.com

DIRECTIONS	Departs from Aswan or Abu Simbel
RATES	$$
ROOMS	55 cabins, 10 suites
FOOD	In keeping with the lavish surroundings
HISTORY	Launched in September 1997
X-FACTOR	Cruising the Nile in style, from era to era

Eine Zeitreise auf dem Nil

Sowohl dem ägyptischen Glauben nach, als auch im alltäglichen Leben, haben Schiffe dort stets eine Doppelrolle gespielt: sie stellten nicht nur ein Transportmittel dar, sondern auch ein Symbol der Hoffnung. Man glaubte, dass der Sonnengott Ra in einem Sonnensschiff quer über den Himmel reiste und es hieß, dass diejenigen, die sich verdient gemacht hatten, den Totengott Osiris nach dem Tode in seiner göttlichen Barke begleiten durften, um ihre unendliche Fahrt anzutreten.

Doch warum auf die nächste Welt warten, wenn Sie solch eine Reise schon heute unternehmen können? An Bord der M.S. Kasr Ibrim oder M.S. Eugenie kann man das Zeitalter der Pharaonen mit dem der Flappers verbinden. Die großartigen Monumente der ersteren breiten sich vor Ihnen am Nilufer aus, während diese prächtigen Dampfschiffe auf dem Nasser-Stausee mit ihren Art Deco Stil an letztere erinnert.

Ein Boot wurde nach der Zitadelle von Kasr Ibrim benannt, einem Relikt aus Nubien, dem Land des Goldes, einem der reichsten Staaten im alten Ägypten. Die einst mächtige Festung steht hier seit ewigen Zeiten. Als man den Assuan Staudamm erbaute, wurden die Tempel von Assuan hierher auf eine höhere Ebene versetzt. Wer hier segelt, sieht die Überreste einer einstmals sagenhaften Vergangenheit. Die Reise führt vorbei an Wundern wie der Straße der Sphinxen bis hin zum großen Höhepunkt, den großen Tempeln von Ramses II in Abu Simbel. Zwar mögen Zeit und Witterung an ihrer Pracht genagt haben, doch ihr Anblick ist unverändert beeindruckend.

An Bord sind Glanz und Gloria noch nicht verblasst. Die prachtvolle Ausstattung der Schiffe ist der Umgebung die sie durchsegelten, angemessen. Von wo aus ließe sich die Großartigkeit Ägyptens besser betrachten, als vom Deck dieser Luxusschiffe?

Buchtipp: »Der Tod auf dem Nil« von Agatha Christie

Un voyage sur le Nil à travers le temps

À la fois moyens de transport et symboles d'espoir, les bateaux jouaient un double rôle dans la croyance et la vie quotidienne des Égyptiens. Leur conviction était que Râ, le dieu soleil, sillonnait le ciel à bord d'un vaisseau solaire et qu'après leur mort, ceux qui en étaient dignes rejoignaient Osiris, le dieu des morts, pour une croisière sans fin sur sa barque divine.

Mais pourquoi attendre d'être dans l'autre monde pour profiter de ce voyage ? Une fois à bord du navire M.S. Kasr Ibrim ou M.S. Eugénie, il est possible de faire le lien entre l'époque des pharaons et celle des garçonnes, ces jeunes filles émancipées des années 20. Les grands monuments des premiers s'offrent au regard sur les rives du Nil et ce splendide bateau à vapeur de style Art Déco qui navigue sur le lac Nasser rappelle les secondes.

L'un des deux bateaux tire son nom de la citadelle de Kasr Ibrim, un vestige de la Nubie, « pays de l'or » et l'un des États les plus riches de l'Égypte antique. La forteresse, autrefois imposante, se dresse ici depuis des milliers d'années. Par la suite, lors de la construction du barrage d'Assouan, d'autres temples furent déplacés sur le site, où le terrain est plus élevé. Ce voyage sur l'eau vous permettra d'admirer ce qui reste de ce fabuleux passé et vous mènera de merveilles telles que l'Allée des sphinx jusqu'aux grands temples de Ramsès II à Abou Simbel, apothéose de votre périple.

Malgré les effets du temps et de la nature qui ont quelque peu terni leur splendeur, ces monuments restent stupéfiants. Votre bateau, lui, a conservé tout son éclat, et sa noblesse est à la hauteur de son environnement. Quel meilleur endroit que le pont de ce luxueux navire pour admirer la magnificence de l'Égypte ?

Livre à emporter : « Mort sur le Nil » d'Agatha Christie

ANREISE	Abfahrt in Assuan oder Abu Simbel
PREIS	$$
ZIMMER	55 Kabinen, 10 Suiten
KÜCHE	So erlesen wie die prächtige Umgebung
GESCHICHTE	1997 vom Stapel gelaufen
X-FAKTOR	Kreuzfahrt entlang des Nils, von einer Ära in die nächste

ACCÈS	Départ d'Assouan ou d'Abou Simbel
PRIX	$$
CHAMBRES	55 cabines, 10 suites
RESTAURATION	Harmonie avec l'environnement somptueux
HISTOIRE	Ouvert en septembre 1997
LES « PLUS »	Une luxueuse croisière sur le Nil pour découvrir les diverses époques de l'Égypte

Natural habitat...

Sarara Luxury Tented Camp, Namunyak Wildlife Conservancy

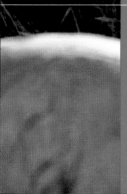

Natural habitat

By night, the sounds of Africa are not like those of other places. A whole range of sounds fills the night here and adds to its mystery. Noises you have not heard before can keep you awake, in the dark. Maybe the raspy breath of some 'thing' nearby, an odd rustle and snap of twigs, or a sudden harsh cry. It is the bush orchestra tuning up – the roar of a lion, a hyena's laugh, or the shrill call of a jackal. In spite of the noise, you will nod off, and wake to early morning birdsong; and perhaps the squeal of a monkey, or the cry of the fish eagle.

A spell in an African bush camp, with the sound of nature around you, and canvas walls, has an effect on all of our senses. Free from the clatter of our normal life, our hearing goes on alert. We are not used to the trumpeting of an elephant; or to the deep silence that can fall here, in such dark nights. The luxury sleeping tents at the Sarara Camp are equipped such that there is no need to go out into that night. Deep in the bush, the camp is in a vast wilderness. Yet herds still come here; of elephants, that is. Sarara is a haven for them too. Lions are locals, along with wild dogs, zebra, giraffe and antelope. They will be at a safe distance; armed guards keep them from being too curious about you. Although difficult to spot, leopards are common; you may hear one near the camp at night. That dry cough just after you dozed off...

Book to pack: "Green City in the Sun" by Barbara Wood

Sarara Luxury Tented Camp
Namunyak
Kenya
Tel: + 254 (20) 643 14 05
Fax + 254 (20) 60 78 93
Email: info@lewa.org
Website: www.lewa.org/sarara.php
www.great-escapes-hotels.com

DIRECTIONS	A 7-hour drive north of Nairobi, or 2 hours from Samburu; or by private air charter from Wilson airport, Nairobi, to Namunyak airstrip
RATES	$$
ROOMS	5 tents for up to 10 people
FOOD	Chefs, not boy scouts, in charge, everything cooked over an open campfire – even the bread
HISTORY	Sarara is part of the Namunyak Wildlife Conservation Trust, working with the tribal community to protect the land and the animals
X-FACTOR	Bush walking and bathing in the waterfalls or pool

Natürlich wohnen

Die Nacht klingt anders in Afrika. Sie ist erfüllt von einer ganzen Reihe von Geräuschen, die ihr etwas geheimnisvoll Mystisches verleihen. Fremde und neuartige Töne werden Sie in der Dunkelheit wach halten. Womöglich das heisere Atmen eines unbekannten Etwas, hier und da das Rascheln und Knacken von Zweigen oder ein plötzlicher rauer Schrei: Der Choral des afrikanischen Busch hebt an – das Brüllen eines Löwen, das Lachen einer Hyäne, oder der schrille Schrei des Schakals. Trotz der Geräuschkulisse werden Sie einschlafen und früh am Morgen vom Gesang der Vögel, dem Quietschen eines Affen oder dem Schrei des Fischadlers erwachen.

Schlafend zwischen Segeltuchwänden und umgeben vom Klang der Natur, berührt ein Aufenthalt in einem afrikanischen Buschcamp all unsere Sinne. Befreit vom Alltagslärm wird unser Gehör wachsam. Weder sind wir an das Trompeten der Elefanten gewohnt, noch an die tiefe Stille, die sich in solchen dunklen Nächten über das Camp breiten kann.

Die Luxuszelte sind so ausgelegt, dass Sie sie in der Nacht nicht verlassen müssen. Das Camp befindet sich tief im Innern des Busches in weiter Wildnis. Hierher kommen auch Elefantenherden, denn Sarara ist auch für sie eine sicherer Hafen. Auch Löwen, wilde Hunde, Zebras, Giraffen und Antilopen leben hier. Doch sie werden in sicherer Entfernung bleiben, während bewaffnete Wächter aufpassen, dass sie Ihnen in ihrer Neugier nicht zu nahe kommen.

Auch Leoparden sind hier zu Hause. Zwar ist es schwer, sie zu entdecken, aber möglicherweise werden Sie nachts, kurz vor dem Einschlummern, seinen kratzigen Husten hören.

Buchtipps: »Die weiße Massai« von Corinne Hofmann
»Rote Sonne, schwarzes Land« von Barbara Wood

L'état de nature

Les bruits qui s'élèvent de la nuit africaine sont uniques. Toute une gamme de sons résonne dans la nuit, ajoutant au mystère. Des bruits jusque-là inconnus peuvent vous tenir éveillé : la respiration rauque et proche d'un animal mystérieux, le bruissement et le craquement des brindilles ou un cri strident et soudain. Ce sont les instruments de l'orchestre de la brousse qui se mettent au diapason : le rugissement du lion, le rire de la hyène ou le cri perçant du chacal. Malgré tout, vous vous laisserez gagner par le sommeil, et c'est le chant matinal des oiseaux qui vous réveillera, peut-être suivi des vociférations des singes ou du cri des aigles pêcheurs. Séjourner dans un camp de brousse africain, entouré des bruits de la nature et de parois en toile, voilà qui met tous les sens en éveil. Libérée de la cacophonie de la vie quotidienne, notre ouïe est en alerte. Elle n'est pas habituée au barrissement des éléphants ou au profond silence qui règne ici une fois la nuit noire tombée.

Les tentes luxueuses de Sarara Camp sont, de toute façon, si bien équipées qu'il n'est nul besoin de s'aventurer dans l'obscurité. Le camp est situé en pleine brousse, au cœur d'une vaste étendue sauvage. Pourtant, les troupeaux – d'éléphants – y viennent en masse. Pour eux aussi Sarara est un havre. Les animaux qui vivent ici en permanence, à savoir les lions, les chiens sauvages, les zèbres, les girafes et les antilopes, sont tenus à distance. Des gardes armés les empêchent de se montrer trop curieux à votre égard.

Même s'il est difficile de les apercevoir, les léopards sont ici courants. Peut-être en entendrez-vous un rôder autour du camp, la nuit, et émettre cette toux sèche caractéristique juste au moment où vous vous assoupirez...

Livre à emporter : « La Massaï blanche » de Corinne Hofmann

ANREISE	Etwa 7-stündige Fahrt nördlich von Nairobi, oder 2-stündig von Samburu; oder vom Wilson Airport, Nairobi, mit einer privaten Chartermaschine nach Namunyak fliegen
PREIS	$$
ZIMMER	5 Zelte für bis zu 10 Personen
KÜCHE	Hier sind echte Köche am Werk – keine Pfadfinder. Alles wird über einem offenen Lagerfeuer zubereitet, sogar das Brot
GESCHICHTE	Sarara gehört zum Namunyak Wildlife Conservation Trust und arbeitet mit der Stammesgemeinschaft zusammen, um das Land und die Tiere zu schützen
X-FAKTOR	Wanderungen durch die Buschlandschaft und Baden in Wasserfälle

ACCÈS	À 7 heures en voiture au nord de Nairobi ou à 2 heures de Samburu. Possibilité d'emprunter un avion-charter privé jusqu'à la piste d'atterrissage de Namunyak
PRIX	$$
CHAMBRES	5 tentes pouvant accueillir jusqu'à 10 personnes
RESTAURATION	Les plats sont élaborés par des chefs cuisiniers et non par des boys scouts. Tout est cuit au feu de camp
HISTOIRE	Sarara fait partie du Namunyak Wildlife Conservation Trust et collabore avec la communauté tribale pour protéger l'environnement et les animaux
LES « PLUS »	Promenades en brousse et baignades en piscine ou sous les chutes d'eau

A bush wilderness...
Il N'gwesi, Northern District

A bush wilderness

For most animals, a key factor for their survival is that they learn, and learn fast, how best to fit in to their surroundings. Those who are adept at this have a better chance of a longer life.

Blending in so well that it is almost camouflaged, Il N'gwesi Lodge looks out over a vast and varied bush landscape. Sweeping views of Northern Kenya are to be seen from its hillside hiding place. At night no other lights shine out; the only sound is the deep chorus of the African bush.

The lodge is an example of a modern style of tourism, one in which the local people play a major part in the preservation of wildlife. Both the wildlife and the people benefit from this. Profits are put back into the local community: Il N'gwesi's success has been such that it now helps support five hundred families and a school. The Lodge is also eco-friendly; only local materials have been used to build it; water is brought in by camels and heated by the sun. Elephant, lion, leopard and antelope turn up to drink at a waterhole of their own nearby; they can be watched, at a discreet distance, from a viewing platform.

A visit to a nearby Maasai manyatta – village – can be arranged, where not only their cultural practices and rituals of daily living are presented, but the hunting skills, traditional rites, and dancing of these proud people are also shared with their guests.

Book to pack: "Green Hills of Africa" by Ernest Hemingway

Il N'gwesi
Northern District
Kenya
Tel: + 254 (20) 64 31 405
Fax: + 254 (20) 60 78 93
E-mail: info@lewa.org
Website: www.lewa.org/ilngwesi_lodge.php
www.great-escapes-hotels.com

DIRECTIONS	A 6-hour drive from Nairobi with access through Lewa or Borana. By private charter direct to Il N'gwesi airstrip. By scheduled service (Air Kenya) daily from Nairobi to Lewa, then a 1.5-hour road transfer
RATES	$$
ROOMS	6 rooms for up to three persons, one of them with a deck where the bed can be rolled out for a night under the stars
FOOD	There is a resident chef, but you need to bring your own food. A shop on site that stocks non-perishable items and drinks
HISTORY	Officially opened in December 1996
X-FACTOR	Choose your guests and contribute to the local community

In tiefster Buschwildnis

Für die meisten Tiere ist es eine überlebensnotwendige Eigenschaft, zu lernen – und zwar schnell zu lernen, wie sie sich am besten ihrer Umgebung anpassen können. Wer am geschicktesten darin ist, hat die größte Chance zu überleben. Die Il N'gwesi Lodge fügt sich so perfekt in ihren Hintergrund ein, dass sie beinahe wie getarnt wirkt.

Von diesem Versteck in den Hügeln eröffnet sich ein umwerfender Blick auf das nördliche Kenia. Das Dunkel der Nacht wird von keiner anderen Lichtquelle gestört; das einzige Geräusch ist der Chor der tiefen Stimmen des afrikanischen Buschs.

Die Lodge ist ein Beispiel für eine moderne Form des Tourismus, in welcher den Einheimischen eine Hauptrolle beim Schutz des Wildparks zukommt. Davon profitieren sowohl Mensch als auch Natur und die Gewinne fließen zurück in die Gemeinschaft. Il N'gwesi ist bisher ein so erfolgreiches Projekt, dass es mittlerweile fünfhundert Familien und eine Schule unterstützt. Außerdem ist die Lodge umweltfreundlich; bei ihrem Bau wurden ausschließlich Materialien aus der Gegend verwendet. Wasser wird von Kamelen gebracht und von der Sonne erwärmt. Elefanten, Löwen, Leoparden und Antilopen kommen zu einem nahegelegenen Wasserloch um ihren Durst zu löschen, wobei man sie von einer Aussichtsplattform aus angemessener Entfernung beobachten kann.

Es ist möglich, einen Besuch in einem benachbarten Massai-Dorf – manyatta – zu organisieren, wo sie ihre Kultur, die Rituale des täglichen Lebens, zur Schau stellen, und wo dieses stolze Volk seine Jagdmethoden, traditionellen Riten und Tänze mit seinen Gästen teilt.

Buchtipp: »Die grünen Hügel Afrikas« von Ernest Hemingway

Au coeur de la brousse

Pour la plupart des animaux, l'élément clé de la survie est d'apprendre rapidement à s'adapter à son environnement. Les plus habiles sont ceux qui ont le plus de chances de vivre plus longtemps.

Se fondant si parfaitement dans son environnement à flanc de coteau qu'il s'en trouve presque camouflé, Il N'gwesi Lodge domine un paysage de brousse vaste et varié et offre une vue panoramique du Nord du Kenya. La nuit, la seule source de lumière alentour est l'éclairage de l'hôtel, et l'unique son, celui de l'intense mélopée de la brousse africaine.

L'hôtel est à l'image du tourisme d'aujourd'hui, dans lequel les autochtones jouent un rôle essentiel en matière de préservation de la faune et de la flore et dont tirent parti tant les animaux que les individus grâce au réinvestissement des bénéfices dans la communauté locale. Le succès d'Il N'gwesi est tel qu'il fait aujourd'hui vivre cinq cent familles et subventionne une école. Il est également respectueux de l'environnement puisque seuls des matériaux locaux ont été utilisés pour sa construction, et l'eau est amenée par chameau et chauffée par les rayons du soleil. Les éléphants, les lions, les léopards et les antilopes viennent se désaltérer à un point d'eau situé à proximité de l'hôtel, et il est possible de les observer à distance respectueuse, depuis une plate-forme prévue à cet effet.

Une visite à un manyatta (village) massaï peut être organisée. Vous y découvrirez les pratiques culturelles et les rituels quotidiens de ce peuple fier, qui partagera avec vous ses techniques de chasse, ses rites traditionnels et ses danses.

Livre à emporter : « Les vertes collines d'Afrique » d'Ernest Hemingway

ANREISE	6-stündige Fahrt von Nairobi über Lewa oder Borana. Sie können mit einer privaten Chartermaschine direkt nach Il N'gwesi oder mit einem Linienflug täglich von Nairobi nach Lewa fliegen, anschließend 1,5-stündige Fahrt zum Anwesen
PREIS	$$
ZIMMER	6 Zimmer für bis zu drei Personen
KÜCHE	Es gibt einen Koch, aber die Zutaten müssen Sie selbst besorgen. Vor Ort ist ein kleiner Laden
GESCHICHTE	Offiziell eröffnet im Jahre 1996
X-FAKTOR	Die Mitbewohner selbst aussuchen und etwas zur lokalen Gemeinschaft beitragen

ACCÈS	À 6 heures en voiture de Nairobi en passant par Lewa ou Borana. Liaison aérienne directe en charter privé entre Nairobi et la piste d'atterrissage d'Il N'gwesi
PRIX	$$
CHAMBRES	6 chambres pouvant accueillir jusqu'à trois personnes, l'une d'entre elles étant équipée d'une terrasse
RESTAURATION	L'hôtel a son propre chef cuisinier, mais vous devrez apporter les ingrédients.
HISTOIRE	Officiellement ouvert en 1996
LES « PLUS »	Choisissez vos compagnons et contribuez à l'esprit collectif local

The lion's den...
Elsa's Kopje, Meru National Park

The lion's den

This is a place for cat lovers – that is of very big, roaring ones. Most of the major felines live here. Not ones you can stroke though. Lions, leopards, and cheetahs prowl this land, a vast space shared with large herds of buffalo, waterbuck, hippo, and eland.

Elsa's Kopje is perched, in pride of place, on top of a rocky outcrop or kopje. The lodge is named after the orphaned lioness that was reared by George and Joy Adamson then returned to the wild. Elsa's story was told in the movie "Born Free".

This is the real 'born free' location, 870 square kilometres of pristine bush as wild, remote and beautiful as it was when the Adamsons were here. Just north of the equator, Meru is Kenya's driest park, with little rainfall, yet it is criss-crossed by rivers and streams flowing down from the nearby mountains. From your private cottage you will have a wide-angle view of the rock and baobab tree landscape. The lodge is sited to showcase the wildlife crossing the plains, and looks across to the foothills of Mount Kenya. There are only eight cottages; their thatched palm roofs and stone walls blend so naturally into the rocky hillside that they are hardly visible from the plains below.

Of course, going on safari is the main pursuit, to view the big cats and other game, like zebra and giraffe. Or you could just stretch out, lazily, by the pool, and wait to be fed.

Book to pack: "Born Free: A Lioness of two Worlds" by Joy Adamson

Elsa's Kopje
Mughwango Hill
Meru National Park
Kenya
Tel + 254 (20) 604 054
Fax + 254 (20) 604 050
E-mail: info@celipeacock.com
Website: www.chelipeacock.com
www.great-escapes-hotels.com

DIRECTIONS	In Meru National Park, access by road, or a 50-minute scheduled flight from Nairobi to Meru Mulika airstrip or charter to camp airstrip
RATES	$$$$
ROOMS	8 double room cottages, 1 family cottage
FOOD	Traditional North Italian cuisine. Yes, Italian
HISTORY	The lodge was opened in 1999
X-FACTOR	The big cats, roaming free in this 'land of the lions'

Ein Ort nicht nur für Raubkatzen

Dies ist ein Ort für Katzenliebhaber, – die von der großen Sorte, die brüllen. Die meisten der wichtigsten Katzenarten sind hier zu Hause. Allerdings keine zum Streicheln. Löwen, Leoparden und Geparden streifen in diesem Land umher; sie teilen sich dieses weite Gebiet mit großen Büffelherden, Wasserböcken, Nilpferden und den Eland-Antilopen. Erhaben thront Elsa's Kopje auf einem Felsvorsprung – Kopje. Benannt wurde die Lodge nach der verwaisten Löwin, die George und Joy Adamson aufgezogen und danach wieder in die Wildnis ausgesetzt hatten. Der Film »Born Free« erzählt Elsas Geschichte. Mit einer Fläche von 870 Quadratkilometern unberührter Buschlandschaft ist dies hier der echte »Born Free« Schauplatz, so wild, abgeschieden und schön wie zu der Zeit, als die Adamsons hier lebten. Meru liegt nur wenig nördlich des Äquators und ist mit seinen geringen Niederschlagsmengen der trockenste Nationalpark Kenias. Dennoch durchziehen Flüsse und Wasserstrassen, die von den nahegelegenen Bergen kommen, das Land. Von Ihrer privaten Hütte aus können Sie den Blick weit über die Landschaft mit ihren Felsformationen und Affenbrotbäumen schweifen lassen. Die Lodge überblickt die Hügel am Fuße des Mount Kenya und wurde so platziert, dass man die Tiere beim Überqueren der Ebene beobachten kann. Es gibt nur acht Hütten hier, und ihre strohgedeckten Dächer fügen sich so natürlich in die felsige Berglandschaft ein, dass man sie von der darunter liegenden Ebene aus kaum ausmachen kann. Wer hierher kommt, ist selbstverständlich vor allem auf Safari und darauf aus, die großen Katzen und andere Raubtiere wie Zebras und Giraffen zu Gesicht zu bekommen. Oder aber Sie machen es sich einfach bequem und liegen faul am Pool, während Sie darauf warten, bis es Essen gibt.

Buchtipp: »Frei Geboren: die Geschichte der Löwin Elsa« von Joy Adamson

L'antre du lion

Cet endroit est fait pour ceux qui aiment les chats. Enfin, les très gros chats. Ceux qui ont tendance à rugir plutôt qu'à miauler. On trouve ici la plupart des grands félins, ceux qu'il n'est, en général, pas conseillé d'essayer de caresser. Les lions, les léopards et les guépards rôdent sur ce vaste territoire, qu'ils partagent avec d'énormes troupeaux de buffles, de cobes, d'hippopotames et d'élands. Perché en haut d'un affleurement rocheux, ou *kopje*, Elsa's Kopje occupe la place d'honneur. À l'origine du nom de l'hôtel, la lionne orpheline élevée par George et Joy Adamson, puis rendue plus tard à la vie sauvage. L'histoire d'Elsa a été racontée dans le film « Né pour être libre ». Le titre du film semble avoir été choisi en fonction de ce lieu : 870 kilomètres carrés de brousse immaculée aussi sauvage, isolée et belle qu'à l'époque des Adamson. Ici, les pluies sont rares. Situé au nord de l'Équateur, Méru est le parc le plus sec du Kenya. Toutefois, de nombreuses rivières et cours d'eau prenant leur source dans les montagnes voisines le traversent. Votre cottage particulier offre une vue panoramique sur un paysage de rochers et de baobabs. L'hôtel, qui fait face aux contreforts du mont Kenya, est une vitrine sur la faune qui sillonne les plaines. Avec leurs toits couverts de palmes et leurs murs de pierre, les huit cottages se fondent si naturellement dans le flanc de la colline rocheuse qu'ils sont presque invisibles depuis la plaine. Bien sûr, l'activité principale de la région est le safari. Elle vous permettra de découvrir les grands félins et les autres animaux, tels que les zèbres et les girafes. Vous pouvez également vous contenter de paresser au bord de la piscine en attendant l'heure du déjeuner.

Livre à emporter : « Elsa, histoire d'une lionne » de Joy Adamson

ANREISE	Liegt im Meru National Park, erreichbar mit dem Wagen, oder per Linienflug von Nairobi nach Meru Mulika Airstrip oder per Charterflug zum Flugplatz des Camps
PREIS	$$$$
ZIMMER	8 Hütten für zwei Personen, 1 Familienhütte
KÜCHE	Traditionelle norditalienische Küche. Jawohl, italienisch!
GESCHICHTE	Die Lodge wurde 1999 eröffnet
X-FAKTOR	Große Katzen, die frei in diesem »Land der Löwen« umherstreifen

ACCÈS	Situé au cœur du Parc national de Méru, accessible par la route, par vol régulier de Nairobi à la piste d'atterrissage de Méru Mulika ou par charter jusqu'au camp
PRIX	$$$$
CHAMBRES	8 cottages pour deux personnes, 1 cottage familial
RESTAURATION	Cuisine traditionnelle du nord de l'Italie. Oui, de l'Italie
HISTOIRE	L'hôtel a ouvert en 1999
LES « PLUS »	Les gros matous en liberté au « pays des lions »

Towering aspirations...
Dodo's Tower, Lake Naivasha

Dodo's Tower, Lake Naivasha

Towering aspirations

Once upon a time, when I was a child, the tale of a girl kept in a tower was one of my favourites. "Rapunzel, Rapunzel, let down your golden hair"; the words the witch, and the prince, called to make her send her lengthy locks down to the ground was a line I loved. However, the tower in the Brothers Grimm story was as bleak as the fable. It had neither door nor staircase, and only one very high window.

This is much more like a fairytale tower, and it's a real one. Dodo's Tower is a whimsical formation on the shores of an enchanting lake; it is one of the most fanciful places to stay in all of Africa. Just its tip can be seen above a forest of acacia trees, yet the rest of it blends quite naturally into the background. At some times of the morning and night, it can trick the eye, morphing more into a tree-trunk than a building. A closer look reveals that a playful yet sure hand, one that loves luxury as much as fantasy, has shaped it. The stylish pagoda is the happy ending to a dream that others can share. It seems to cast a benign spell over all who come here.

Having a wooden spire in the middle of the landscape does not seem to phase the creatures that share this setting. Hippos and giraffes, or pelicans and flamingos seldom play a part in fables; yet they can be seen far below from the verandas of this imaginative place.

Books to pack: Several, so that you need not come down...
"The Lord of the Rings. The Two Towers" by J.R.R. Tolkien
"The Seven Story Tower" by Curtiss Hoffman
"The Ebony Tower" by John Fowles
"Child of Happy Valley" by Juanita Carberry

Dodo's Tower	
P.O. Box 24397	
Nairobi	
Kenya	
Tel: + 254 (20) 57 46 89	
Fax: + 254 (20) 56 49 45	
E-mail: mellitera@swiftkenya.com	
Website: www.hippo-pointkenya.com	
www.great-escapes-hotels.com	

DIRECTIONS	A 20-minute charter flight from Nairobi to Naivasha airstrip and then a 40-minute drive to the estate. By road, the estate is a 1.5-hour drive north west from Nairobi
RATES	$$$$
ROOMS	5, on four floors, with a meditation room at the very top
FOOD	Magical menus conjured up by a French wizard
HISTORY	Built in the early 1990s on the same estate as Hippo Point House
X-FACTOR	The chance to be in a fairytale of your own

Ein Turm wie aus einem Märchen

Es war einmal ein Märchen... als ich ein Kind war, gehörte die Geschichte von dem Mädchen, das in einem Turm gefangen gehalten wurde, zu meinen Lieblingserzählungen. »Rapunzel, Rapunzel, lass dein goldenes Haar herunter.« Ich liebte diese Stelle, wenn die Hexe und der Prinz jene Worte riefen, damit das Mädchen seine langen Locken zum Boden hinabließ. Trotzdem – der Turm in der Geschichte der Gebrüder Grimm ist so düster wie die Erzählung selbst. Er hatte weder eine Türe noch eine Treppe und nur ein einziges, sehr hoch gelegenes Fenster.

Der Turm, von dem hier die Rede ist, sieht aus wie ein Märchenturm, doch er ist echt! Dodo's Tower ist ein skurriles Gebäude am Ufer eines bezaubernden Sees, einem der fantastischsten Orte in Afrika. Man kann nur seine Spitze aus einem Akazienwald herausragen sehen; der übrige Teil fügt sich ganz natürlich in die Umgebung ein. Manchmal, im frühen Morgen- oder Abendlicht, ähnelt der Turm, wie durch eine optische Täuschung, eher einem alten Baumstamm als einem Gebäude. Bei genauerem Hinsehen wird jedoch deutlich, dass dies ein spielerisches, aber dennoch exakt geplantes Werk ist, erbaut von jemandem, der Luxus und Fantasie gleichermaßen liebt. Die stilvolle Pagode ist wie ein wahrgewordener Traum und scheint jeden mit einer Art gutem Zauber zu belegen. Der hölzerne Turm inmitten der Landschaft stört die dort lebenden Tiere offenbar keineswegs. Nilpferde und Giraffen, Pelikane und Flamingos kommen in Märchen eher selten vor. Doch von seiner Veranda aus kann man sie weit unter sich sehen.

Buchtipps: Gleich mehrere, damit Sie nicht vom Turm herunterkommen müssen...

»Der Herr der Ringe. Die zwei Türme« von J.R.R. Tolkien
»Letzte Tage in Kenia. Meine Kindheit in Afrika« von Juanita Carberry
»Sehnsucht nach Kenia. Ein afrikanisches Reisetagebuch« von Hannelore Kornherr

Au-dessus des girafes

Lorsque j'étais enfant, l'un de mes contes favoris était celui narrant l'histoire d'une jeune fille enfermée dans une tour. « Rapunzel, Rapunzel, détache tes cheveux blonds. » J'adorais ces mots que la sorcière et le prince adressaient à la jeune fille pour la convaincre de laisser tomber sa chevelure jusqu'au sol. Pourtant, la tour du conte des frères Grimm, sans porte ni escalier et dotée d'une unique et haute fenêtre, était aussi lugubre que la fable elle-même.

Dodo's Tower est plus conforme à l'image habituelle d'une tour de conte de fées, et elle est bien réelle. Construction insolite installée sur les rives d'un lac enchanteur, il s'agit de l'un des hôtels les plus originaux de toute l'Afrique. Seul son sommet dépasse d'une forêt d'acacias, le reste de son architecture se fondant naturellement dans le paysage. À certaines heures du matin et du soir, vos yeux peuvent vous jouer des tours et donner à l'édifice l'apparence d'un tronc d'arbre. Mais en y regardant de plus près, on s'aperçoit qu'il a été façonné par une main espiègle mais habile, amatrice de luxe tout autant que de fantaisie. L'élégante pagode est l'heureux dénouement d'un rêve que les visiteurs sont invités à partager, et tous sont immédiatement envoûtés.

La présence de cette flèche de bois au milieu du paysage ne semble pas troubler les créatures qui partagent le territoire. Les fables ne mettent jamais en scène les hippopotames, les girafes, les pélicans ou les flamants roses. Ici, installés dans la véranda de ce lieu plein d'imagination, vous pourrez toutefois les voir évoluer loin en contrebas.

Livres à emporter : Plusieurs suggestions, pour ne pas avoir à redescendre sur terre...

« Le Seigneur des Anneaux. Les Deux Tours » J.R.R. Tolkien
« La Tour d'Ébène » de John Fowles
« Valjoie » de Nathaniel Hawthorne

ANREISE	Mit einer privaten Chartermaschine etwa 20 Minuten von Nairobi nach Naivasha, anschließend 40-minütige Fahrt zum Anwesen. Mit dem Wagen 1,5-stündige Fahrt nordwestlich von Nairobi
PREIS	$$$$
ZIMMER	5 Zimmer auf vier Stockwerken, im obersten ein Meditationsraum
KÜCHE	Magische Menüs, von einem französischen Chef gezaubert
GESCHICHTE	In den frühen 1990ern erbaut. Befindet sich auf dem selben Grundstück wie Hippo Point House
X-FAKTOR	Die Chance, ein einer Fabel zu leben

ACCÈS	En avion, vol Nairobi-Naivasha d'une durée de 20 minutes, puis 40 minutes en voiture. Au nord-ouest de Nairobi, à 1H30 en voiture
PRIX	$$$$
CHAMBRES	5, réparties sur quatre étages, avec salle de méditation au dernier
RESTAURATION	Menus enchanteurs concoctés par un chef français
HISTOIRE	Construite au début des années 1990 sur la même propriété que Hippo Point House
LES « PLUS »	Un véritable conte de fées

Vestiges of England...
Hippo Point House, Lake Naivasha

Vestiges of England

There are no fairies at the bottom of this English garden.
Instead, the real reverse of those fantasy and lighter-than-air
creatures lives here. Hundreds of "river horses", as the
Greeks once called them, or hippopotami, as we know them
now, are just outside the fence. They like to eat the flowers,
so they must be kept out.

Hippo Point House is set in a garden of fragrant roses
and verdant lawns; a mock-Tudor manor in classic grounds
leading down to a pretty lake.

So far, it is a scene typical in an English landscape, but
it is in the heart of Kenya's Great Rift Valley. That makes
the livestock to be seen here even more of a contrast to the
house. The lovely old home was built in the 1930s in the
romantic style popular in England then. Its original owners
had been transplanted to 'deepest darkest Africa'; to them,
this house and garden was a token of their native land thousands of miles away. Years later it was found in ruins, but
reinvented as a fine guesthouse. Under its gabled roof, the
elegant rooms are furnished with antiques, more memories
of a distant Europe. Inside, it could still be a corner of
England. Once outside, the difference is of course clear.
This is a sanctuary; giraffe, hippo, antelope, zebra, and
leopards, and hundreds of different sorts of birds live here.
The sounds, and scents, of Africa and England are worlds
apart.

Books to pack: "White Mischief" by James Fox
"The Hippopotamus" by Stephen Fry

Hippo Point House
P. O. Box 1852
Naivasha
Kenya
Tel: + 254 (733) 333 014
E-mail: hippo-pt@africaonline.co.ke
Website: www.hippo-pointkenya.com
www.great-escapes-hotels.com

DIRECTIONS	By air, a 20-minute charter from Nairobi to Naivasha air-strip, and then a 40-minute drive to the estate. By road, a 1.5-hour drive north west from Nairobi
RATES	$$$$
ROOMS	8 rooms for up to 14 people
FOOD	French influenced
HISTORY	Built in the 1930s, and much later Dodo's Tower, the folly, was built on the same property by the present owners
X-FACTOR	Seeming to have a foot in two countries

Englische Reminiszenzen

Elfen, die ja angeblich in jedem echten englischen Garten zu finden sind, gibt es hier zwar keine, dafür aber das genaue Gegenteil dieser zarten Fantasiegestalten, die leichter sind als Luft. Direkt hinter dem Zaun leben Hunderte von Flusspferden oder Hippopotami, wie sie schon die alten Griechen nannten. Der Zaun soll sie davon abhalten die Blumen zu fressen. Hippo Point House liegt inmitten eines duftenden, grünen Rosengartens. Es wurde einem Tudorgut nachempfunden, und seine klassische Parkanlage führt zu einem kleinen See hinab. Bis hierher klingt dies alles nach einem typisch englischen Schauplatz, doch er liegt im Herzen von Kenias Great Rift Valley. Die Tiere, die man hier beobachten kann, bilden dadurch einen umso stärkeren Kontrast zu dem Haus.

Das bezaubernde alte Gebäude wurde in den 1930er Jahren erbaut – gemäß dem romantischen Stil, der zu jener Zeit in England so beliebt war. Seine ursprünglichen Besitzer waren gezwungen gewesen, in das »tiefste, schwärzeste Afrika« zu ziehen, deshalb stellten für sie dieses Haus und der Garten eine Art Verbindungsglied dar zu ihrer Tausende von Meilen weit entfernten Heimat. Jahre später, das Haus war mittlerweile eine Ruine, entdeckte man es neu und baute es zu einem Hotel um. Unter seinem Giebeldach befinden sich elegante Räume, die – ausgestattet mit Antiquitäten – Erinnerungen an das ferne Europa wachrufen.

Die Innenräume könnten tatsächlich in irgendeinem Winkel Englands liegen. Doch sobald man aus dem Gebäude heraustritt, wird der Unterschied selbstverständlich sofort offensichtlich: Dies ist ein unberührtes Wildreservat in welchem Giraffen, Flusspferde, Antilopen, Zebras, Leoparden, sowie Hunderte verschiedener Vogelarten leben. Zwischen den Geräuschen und Gerüchen Afrikas und Englands liegen wahrhaftig Welten.

Buchtipps: »Weißes Verhängnis« von James Fox
»Das Nilpferd« von Stephen Fry

Vestiges d'Angleterre

Au fond de ce jardin anglais, tout droit sorties d'un conte de fées, évoluent des créatures aux antipodes de ces êtres fantastiques et gracieux. Des centaines d'hippopotames, ou « chevaux de rivière » comme les appelaient les Grecs, vivent en effet juste de l'autre côté de la clôture. Étant donné leur goût prononcé pour les fleurs, l'entrée du site leur est interdite.

Hippo Point House, imitation d'un manoir Tudor, est installé sur un domaine d'agencement classique descendant jusqu'à un lac charmant, au milieu d'un jardin de roses odorantes et de pelouses verdoyantes.

Ce cadre, qui s'apparente à un paysage anglais typique, se trouve en réalité au cœur de la grande vallée du Rift, au Kenya, d'où le fort contraste entre la propriété et la faune alentour. Cette jolie vieille demeure fut construite dans les années trente dans le style romantique alors en vogue en Angleterre. Pour ses premiers propriétaires, transplantés « au plus profond de l'Afrique noire », la maison et son jardin symbolisaient leur pays natal, à des milliers de kilomètres de là. Des années plus tard, la bâtisse, alors en ruine, fut restaurée et retrouva une nouvelle vie en tant que pension de famille raffinée. Protégées par un toit à double pente, les chambres élégantes sont meublées d'antiquités, autres souvenirs d'une Europe lointaine. Encore aujourd'hui, une fois à l'intérieur, on pourrait se croire en Angleterre. Mais dès que l'on met le pied dehors, la différence saute aux yeux : des girafes, des hippopotames, des antilopes, des zèbres, des léopards et des centaines d'espèces d'oiseaux vivent dans cette réserve naturelle. Et les sons et les parfums de l'Afrique n'ont rien à voir avec ceux de l'Angleterre.

Livres à emporter : « Je rêvais de l'Afrique » de Kuki Gallmann
« L'hippopotame » de Stephen Fry

ANREISE	Ein etwa 20-minütiger Flug mit einer privaten Chartermaschine von Nairobi nach Naivasha. Von dort aus 40-minütige Fahrt zum Anwesen. Mit dem Wagen 1,5- stündige Fahrt nordwestlich von Nairobi	
PREIS	$$$$	
ZIMMER	8 Zimmer für bis zu 14 Personen	
KÜCHE	Französisch angehaucht	
GESCHICHTE	Erbaut in den 1930er Jahren; auf dem selben Grundstück errichteten die heutigen Besitzer viel später Dodo's Tower	
X-FAKTOR	Zwei Kulturen an einem Ort	

ACCÈS	Trajet de 20 minutes en avion de Nairobi jusqu'à la piste d'atterrissage de Naivasha, puis 40 minutes en voiture jusqu'à la propriété. À 1H30 au nord-ouest de Nairobi en voiture	
PRIX	$$$$	
CHAMBRES	8 chambres pouvant accueillir jusqu'à 14 personnes	
RESTAURATION	Influences françaises	
HISTOIRE	Construit dans les années 30. Bien plus tard, les propriétaires actuels firent édifier une folie, la Tour de Dodo, sur le même domaine	
LES « PLUS »	Impression d'être dans deux pays différents à la fois	

Visits from giraffes...
The Giraffe Manor, near Nairobi

Visits from giraffes

This elegant house was here before the giraffes; but luckily, it was constructed as a two-storey building, so that now the statuesque creatures can be fed at a height that best suits them. There are some benefits in being so tall. Gazing through the upper windows as they stroll by is a usual bent for them, though it might be surprising for guests.

The Giraffe Manor is home to several of these bizarre yet beautiful animals. The ones that live here in the acres of forest are rare Rothschild giraffes, descendants of what were once an endangered species. In the 1970s, the house owners set up the African Fund for Endangered Wildlife: a name that was soon and aptly shortened to AFEW. They transferred five baby giraffes to their property, with the result that they are on record as being the only people to have successfully brought up wild giraffes. Those are now grown-up with babies of their own.

There is a human story here too. One of the bedrooms is furnished with pieces that Tania Blixen, author of "Out of Africa", gave to the owners when she left Kenya. And upstairs, in the hall, are the bookcases that the love of her life, Denys Finch-Hatton, made for her.

The world's tallest animal does not have the sole advantage of height here; the snow capped peak of Kilimanjaro, the highest mountain in Africa, can be seen in the distance. "African legend insists that man arrived on earth by sliding down the giraffe's neck from Heaven"... Betty Leslie Melville, co-founder with Jock Leslie-Melville of AFEW.

Book to pack: "Zarafa" by Michael Allin

The Giraffe Manor
P.O. Box 15004
Langata, 00509 Nairobi
Kenya
Tel: + 254 (20) 89 10 78
Fax: + 254 (20) 89 09 49
E-mail: giraffem@kenyaweb.com
Website: www.giraffemanor.com
www.great-escapes-hotels.com

DIRECTIONS	20 km/12 m south west of Nairobi; 20 minutes from the airport
RATES	$$$$
ROOMS	6 bedrooms with bathrooms
FOOD	The chef focuses on providing for the guests, not the giraffes
HISTORY	Built in 1932
X-FACTOR	Feeding the giraffes from your upper-storey window, or at even closer quarters

Giraffen zu Besuch

Dieses elegante Haus stand bereits hier, bevor die Giraffen da waren; doch glücklicherweise wurde es zweistöckig konstruiert, so dass die stattlich hohen Tiere aus optimaler Höhe gefüttert werden können. So groß zu sein, hat einige Vorteile. Und während es für die Hotelgäste durchaus überraschend sein mag, ist es für die Giraffen ganz normal, dass sie einen Blick durch die oberen Fenster werfen, wenn Sie draußen vorbeistolzieren. Giraffe Manor beheimatet gleich mehrere dieser bizarren und doch gleichzeitig so schönen Kreaturen. Die Tiere, die in diesem mehrere Morgen großen Waldgebiet leben, gehören zur Spezies der seltenen Rothschild Giraffe, und sind somit Nachkommen einer einst vom Aussterben bedrohten Art.

In den 1970er Jahren riefen die Besitzer des Hauses den Afrikanischen Fond Existenzbedrohter Wildtierarten ins Leben (»African Fund for Endangered Wildlife«), ein Name, der bald darauf kurz und prägnant zu AFEW abgekürzt wurde. Sie siedelten fünf Babygiraffen auf ihrem Grundstück an und sind seither bekannt dafür, die einzigen Menschen zu sein, die es jemals geschafft haben, wilde Giraffen großzuziehen.

Hier gibt es jedoch auch eine Geschichte von Menschen zu erzählen. Eines der Schafzimmer wurde mit Möbeln ausgestattet, die Tania Blixen, die Autorin von »Out of Africa«, den Besitzern schenkte, als sie Kenia verließ. Und oben, in der Halle, stehen die Bücherregale, die Denys Finch-Hatton, die Liebe ihres Lebens, für sie gezimmert hatte.

Das größte Tier der Welt ist nicht das einzige, was hier einen Anspruch auf die Bezeichnung groß oder hoch erheben kann: in der Ferne kann man die schneebedeckte Kuppe des höchsten Berges in Afrika erkennen – die Spitze des Kilimandscharo.

»Die afrikanische Welterschaffungslegende besagt, dass der Mensch vom Himmel auf die Erde kam, indem er einen Giraffenhals hinabrutschte.« Betty Leslie-Melville, Mitbegründerin von AFEW gemeinsam mit Jock Leslie-Melville.

Buchtipp: »Zarafa« von Michael Allin

Visites amicales des girafes

Cet élégant édifice existait avant l'arrivée des girafes. Fort heureusement, l'architecte avait prévu deux étages, et l'on peut aujourd'hui nourrir ces créatures sculpturales depuis une hauteur appropriée. Il y a des avantages à être grand.

Les girafes sont curieuses et ont tendance à venir regarder longuement au travers les fenêtres les plus hautes lors de leurs déambulations, même si cela peut prendre au dépourvu les clients de l'hôtel.

Giraffe Manor abrite plusieurs de ces étranges et magnifiques animaux. Les girafes qui vivent ici, dans l'immense forêt, sont des animaux rares, les girafes Rothschild, descendantes d'une espèce autrefois en voie d'extinction. Dans les années 70, les propriétaires fondèrent l'African Fund for Endangered Wildlife (Fonds africain pour les espèces menacées), rapidement abrégé en AFEW, et transférèrent cinq girafons dans leur propriété. C'est la seule expérience réussie au monde d'un élevage de girafes sauvages, aujourd'hui adultes et à leur tour mamans.

L'homme a aussi apporté sa pierre à l'histoire de ce lieu. L'une des chambres est en effet garnie d'objets donnés par Tania Blixen, l'auteur de « La ferme africaine » (« Out of Africa ») avant son départ du Kenya. En outre, dans le hall du premier étage se trouvent les bibliothèques fabriquées pour elle par l'amour de sa vie, Denys Finch-Hatton.

L'animal le plus grand du monde n'a pas le monopole de la hauteur : vous apercevrez à l'horizon les sommets enneigés du Kilimandjaro, la montagne la plus haute d'Afrique.

« La légende africaine veut que l'Homme soit arrivé du paradis sur la terre en glissant le long du cou d'une girafe... » Betty Leslie Melville, cofondatrice de l'AFEW avec Jock Leslie-Melville.

Livre à emporter : « La girafe de Charles X » de Michael Allin

ANREISE	20 km südwestlich von Nairobi entfernt; 20 Minuten vom Flughafen	
PREIS	$$$$	
ZIMMER	6 Zimmer mit Bad	
KÜCHE	Der Koch konzentriert sich darauf, die Gäste zu verwöhnen, nicht die Giraffen	
GESCHICHTE	Erbaut im Jahre 1932	
X-FAKTOR	Füttern Sie Giraffen vom Fenster Ihres Zimmers im ersten Stock aus, oder kommen Sie Ihnen sogar noch näher	

ACCÈS	À 20 km au sud-ouest de Nairobi et à 20 minutes de l'aéroport
PRIX	$$$$
CHAMBRES	6 chambres avec salle de bain
RESTAURATION	Le chef cuisinier se consacre aux clients et non aux girafes !
HISTOIRE	Construit en 1932
LES « PLUS »	Vous nourrirez les girafes depuis votre chambre à l'étage ou depuis la terre ferme si vous le souhaitez

Smell the coffee...
Ngong House, near Nairobi

Smell the coffee

Those with a sharp sense of smell might detect a lingering aroma here: the rich scent of coffee. Or perhaps only those with a keen mind's eye may think it so. It would be a reminder of the past owner and a use this land was once put to: as a coffee farm, whose mistress was Tania Blixen. Ngong House is on what was the famous writer's estate.
"I had a farm in Africa, at the foot of the Ngong Hills."
This opening line from her book is a spare prologue to the story of the land she grew to love and describe so expressively. "The Equator runs across these highlands, in the daytime you felt as though you had got high up, near to the sun, but the early mornings and evenings were limpid and restful, and the nights were cold."
There is height here indeed, in the landscape and in the lodgings. Tree houses are the rooms with a view at Ngong House; not the usual style though. These are more whimsical, on two levels, with plump four-poster beds, doors made from old Arab ships, stained glass windows, a fireplace, bar, even a kitchen. Each one has its own character. The furniture might be made of camphor wood, or of old railway hardwood sleepers, or the intricate hand-carved chairs of the island of Lamu. The verandah is a place to bask in the sun, drink gin, tea, or coffee, and watch the bird life fly by or gaze at the misty Ngong Hills.
"The Mountain of Ngong stretches in a long ridge from north to south, and is crowned with four noble peaks like immovable darker blue waves against the sky."
Book to pack: "Out of Africa" by Tania Blixen

Ngong House
P.O. Box 24963
00502 Nairobi
Kenya
Tel: + 254 (20) 891-856 / 890 140 / 891 296
Fax: + 254 (20) 890 674
E-mail: enquiries@roveafrica.com
Website: www.ngonghouse.com
www.great-escapes-hotels.com

DIRECTIONS	A 20-minute drive south from the centre of Nairobi
RATES	$$$$
ROOMS	5 tree houses, 2 rooms in the main house
FOOD	High quality to go with the lofty location
HISTORY	Opened in 1995
X-FACTOR	The feeling of a remote African outpost, not far from the city

Kaffeeduft liegt in der Luft

Wer über einen ausgeprägten Geruchssinn verfügt, mag hier ein feines Aroma in der Luft bemerken: den Geruch von Kaffee. Vielleicht bilden sich das aber auch nur diejenigen ein, die eine starke Vorstellungskraft haben. Der Geruch erinnert daran, wer hier einst die Besitzerin war, und wofür das Land zu jener Zeit genutzt wurde: dies ist die Kaffeeplantage, über die einst Tania Blixen Herrin war.

Ngong House wurde auf dem Grund erbaut, der damals der berühmten Schriftstellerin gehörte. »Ich hatte eine Farm in Afrika am Fuß der Ngong Hügel.« Dieser erste Satz ihres Romans ist eine recht spärlich klingende Einleitung zu der Geschichte des Landes, das sie so lieben lernte und später so eindrucksvoll beschrieb. »Der Äquator verläuft durch dieses Hochland. Tagsüber fühlte man sich, als wäre man hoch hinaufgekommen, in die Nähe der Sonne, aber die frühe Morgenzeit und die Abende waren klar und friedlich und die Nächte waren kalt«.

Hoch hinaus geht es hier tatsächlich, sowohl was die Landschaft, als auch was die Unterkunft betrifft. Zimmer mit Ausblick, damit sind hier, in Ngong House, Baumhäuser gemeint, wenn auch keine gewöhnlichen. Die zweistöckigen Baumhäuser sind skurrile Bauwerke mit mächtigen 4-pfostigen Betten, Türen, die aus arabischem Schiffsholz gefertigt sind, bunten Glasfenstern, einer offenen Feuerstelle, einer Bar und sogar einer Küche. Jede Hütte hat ihren eigenen Charakter. Die Einrichtung besteht zum Teil aus Kampferholz, wie die Hartholzbetten aus alten Eisenbahnschlafwagen oder die aufwändig handgeschnitzten Stühle von der Insel Lamu.

Auf der Veranda kann man in der Sonne liegen, während man einen Gin, Tee oder Kaffee zu sich nimmt und dabei die Vögel beobachtet, oder auf die in leichtem Nebel liegenden Ngong Hügel blickt.

»Der Ngong Berg erstreckt sich in einem langen Rücken von Nord nach Süd und ist mit vier edlen Gipfeln gekrönt, die sich wie unbewegliche, dunkle blaue Wellen vom Himmel abheben.«

Buchtipp: »Out of Africa« von Tania Blixen

L'ivresse de café

Ceux qui ont un odorat développé seront peut-être capables de détecter ici un arôme persistant : le parfum enivrant du café. Ou peut-être seules les personnes douées d'une imagination fertile seront-elles en mesure de percevoir ces effluves qui évoquent l'ancienne propriétaire, Tania Blixen, et l'usage que l'on faisait autrefois de cette terre : une plantation de café.

Ngong House se trouve sur un domaine qui appartenait au célèbre écrivain. « J'avais une ferme en Afrique, au pied des montagnes Ngong. » La première phrase de son livre est une introduction laconique à l'histoire de cette terre que Tania Blixen apprit à aimer et qu'elle décrivit de façon si expressive. « L'Équateur s'étend le long de ces montagnes. Pendant la journée, on avait l'impression de s'élever très haut et de toucher le soleil, mais l'aube et le soir étaient limpides et paisibles, et les nuits étaient froides. »

La hauteur est en effet bien présente ici, dans le paysage comme dans les habitations. À Ngong House, les chambres avec vue sont des maisonnettes perchées dans les arbres. Leur style est unique et insolite. Elles s'étendent sur deux niveaux et sont dotées de lits à baldaquin moelleux, de portes fabriquées à partir d'anciens vaisseaux arabes, de fenêtres à vitraux, d'une cheminée, d'un bar et même d'une cuisine. Chaque chambre a son caractère propre. Le mobilier est en bois de camphrier ou fabriqué à partir de traverses en bois dur d'anciennes voies de chemin de fer ou de chaises provenant de l'île de Lamu dont les gravures complexes ont été exécutées à la main.

La véranda est idéale pour se prélasser au soleil, boire un verre de gin, une tasse de thé ou de café en regardant les oiseaux dans le ciel ou les montagnes Ngong couvertes de brume.

« La longue chaîne des montagnes Ngong s'étend du nord au sud. Elle est couronnée de quatre nobles pics formant autant de vagues bleu sombre contre le ciel. »

Livre à emporter : « La ferme africaine » de Tania Blixen

ANREISE	20-minütige Autofahrt südlich vom Zentrum in Nairobi entfernt
PREIS	$$$$
ZIMMER	5 Baumhäuser, 2 Zimmer im Haupthaus
KÜCHE	«Hohe» Küche, passend zur hohen Behausung
GESCHICHTE	Eröffnet im Jahre 1995
X-FAKTOR	Atmosphäre wie in einem weit abgelegenen Außenposten Afrikas, nicht weit von der Stadt entfernt

ACCÈS	À 20 minutes en voiture du centre de Nairobi, par le sud
PRIX	$$$$
CHAMBRES	5 maisonnettes dans les arbres, 2 chambres dans le bâtiment principal
RESTAURATION	Excellente, en accord avec la noblesse du lieu
HISTOIRE	Ouvert en 1995
LES « PLUS »	Atmosphère d'un avant-poste africain isolé, tout près de la ville

Trading places...
Peponi Hotel, Lamu

Peponi Hotel, Lamu

Trading places

There is a lovely lazy mood here, so you should stay away if you want a place that is full of hustle and bustle. That is not to say that there is nothing to do; on the contrary, but it can be done at the pace you choose.

The island of Lamu has been in a time warp for three hundred years. Since the Oman Sultan moved to Zanzibar, life has continued much as it was then. There are still no cars here; the narrow streets of the ancient town are very much as they were. One of the first trading outposts on the East African coast, it is a heady mix of Arabic Indian and African cultures. Classic boats common to this part of the world – dhows – still set sail each day as they have for centuries. There is a small family owned and run inn here, one that has long been a favourite escape of those in the know.

Set on a headland, the Peponi Hotel is at a halfway point between two worlds. In one direction are the sounds and scenes of Lamu Old Town: white stone houses with intricately carved doorways, hidden courtyards, and tiny shops; and the haunting call to prayer from the mosques. In the other, a curve of beach – said to be crowded if ten people are on it – miles of white sand edged with turquoise water. You can sit and swing, rapt in a time zone of your own, look out at the Indian Ocean, sip a Lamu lime juice and question why you were ever in a rush.

In Africa, it is said that "Even time takes its time." Robert Levine

Books to pack: "Mr Bigstuff and the Goddess of Charm" by Fiona Sax Ledger

"A Geography of Time" by Robert Levine

Peponi Hotel	
P.O. Box 24	
Lamu	
Kenya	
Tel: + 254 (42) 63 34 21	
Fax: + 254 (42) 63 30 29	
E-mail: peponi@pepomi-lamu.com	
Website: www.peponi-lamu.com	
www.great-escapes-hotels.com	

DIRECTIONS	A short boat ride from Lamu Town after a flight from Nairobi or Mombasa
RATES	$$
ROOMS	24, all rooms have ocean views
FOOD	The speciality is seafood, with ginger, lime and garlic – mangrove crabs, warm water lobster, squid, giant prawns and fish of all varieties. A Swahili menu is also available
HISTORY	Opened in 1967, still owned and run by the same family
X-FACTOR	At 2 degrees below the Equator, there seems to be more time here

Handelsaußenposten

Hier herrscht eine liebenswert faule Atmosphäre, und wenn Sie auf der Suche nach permanent geschäftigem Treiben sind, sollten Sie diesem Ort besser fernbleiben. Das heißt aber nicht, dass es hier nichts zu tun gäb, im Gegenteil, – aber die Geschwindigkeit, mit der Sie es tun, bestimmen Sie ganz einfach selbst. Seit nunmehr dreihundert Jahren befindet sich die Insel Lamu in einer Art Zeitschleife. Seitdem der Sultan von Oman nach Sansibar gezogen ist, hat das Leben hier ziemlich unverändert seinen Lauf genommen. Der erste Handelsaußenposten an der ostafrikanischen Küste ist eine eigenwillige Mischung aus arabischer, indischer und afrikanischer Kultur. Die traditionellen Boote, wie sie in diesem Teil der Welt üblich sind, die Dhows, setzen täglich ihre Segel, so wie sie es Jahrhunderte lang getan haben.

Hier gibt es eine Pension in Familienbesitz, die schon seit langer Zeit der Lieblingszufluchtsort all jener ist, die das Glück haben, von ihrer Existenz zu wissen. Das Peponi Hotel, das auf einer Landzunge gelegen ist, markiert eine Art Scheidepunkt zwischen zwei Welten. Auf der einen Seite spielt sich das Leben von Lamus Altstadt mit all seinen typischen Geräuschen ab: weiße Steinhäuser mit aufwendig geschnitzten Eingangstüren, verborgenen Innenhöfen, winzige Läden, und der Aufruf zum Gebet schallt durchdringend von den Moscheen. Auf der anderen Seite der Strand – Meilen von weißem Sand begrenzt nur vom türkisfarbenen Wasser. Dieser Strand gilt übrigens als überfüllt, wenn sich mehr als zehn Menschen dort aufhalten.

Hier kann man sitzen, die Seele baumeln lassen – in seine eigene Zeitzone entrückt – während man auf den Indischen Ozean hinausblickt, Limettensaft aus Lamu schlürft und sich darüber wundert, warum man je so in Eile war.

»In Afrika sagt man, dass sogar die Zeit ihre Zeit braucht.«
Robert Levine

Buchtipps: »Eine Landkarte der Zeit. Wie Kulturen mit Zeit umgehen« von Robert Levine
»Nirgendwo in Afrika« von Stefanie Zweig

Le comptoir oublié

Il règne ici une ambiance délicieusement nonchalante. Si vous recherchez l'agitation et un tourbillon d'activité, cet endroit n'est pas pour vous. Cela ne veut pas dire pour autant qu'ici il n'y a rien à faire. Bien au contraire. Seulement, c'est vous qui décidez du rythme. Sur l'île de Lamu, le temps semble avoir suspendu son vol il y a trois cents ans.

Depuis que le sultan d'Oman est parti pour Zanzibar, la vie n'a pratiquement pas changé. Il n'y a toujours pas de voitures, et les rues étroites de la vieille ville n'ont subi que peu de modifications. Lamu, l'un des premiers postes d'approvisionnement de la côte de l'Afrique orientale, est un mélange enivrant de culture arabe, indienne et africaine. Les *boutres*, embarcations typiques de cette partie du monde, prennent la mer tous les jours, et ce depuis des siècles.

Lamu abrite une petite auberge familiale qu'affectionnent les rares privilégiés qui la connaissent. Dressé sur un promontoire, l'hôtel Peponi est à mi-chemin entre deux mondes : d'un côté, le spectacle et les sons du vieux Lamu, avec ses maisons en pierre blanche aux portes décorées de gravures complexes, ses cours cachées, ses minuscules échoppes et l'appel lancinant à la prière en provenance des mosquées ; de l'autre, une plage courbe, que les habitants jugent comble dès que plus de dix personnes y posent le pied, et la mer turquoise bordée par des kilomètres de sable blanc.

Vous pouvez vous asseoir, savourer le moment, et passer le temps, un temps qui n'appartient qu'à vous, à admirer l'Océan Indien, en sirotant un jus de citron vert de Lamu et en vous demandant ce qui a bien pu vous obliger à vous presser par le passé.

On dit en Afrique que « même le temps prend son temps. »
Robert Levine.

Livres à emporter : « Une enfance africaine » de Stefanie Zweig
« Les Swahili entre Afrique et Arabie » de Françoise Le Guennec-Coppens et Patricia Caplan

ANREISE	Nach einem Flug von Nairobi oder Mombasa, kurze Bootsfahrt von Lamu Stadt
PREIS	$$
ZIMMER	24 Zimmer, alle mit Meeresblick
KÜCHE	Spezialität des Hauses sind Fisch und Meeresfrüchte mit Ingwer und Knoblauch. Außerdem gibt es Swahili-Menüs
GESCHICHTE	Eröffnet im Jahre 1967, seitdem im Besitz derselben Familie, die das Hotel auch führt
X-FAKTOR	2 Grad unterhalb des Äquators scheint es einfach mehr Zeit zu geben

ACCÈS	En avion jusqu'à Lamu depuis Nairobi ou Mombasa, puis court trajet en bateau
PRIX	$$
CHAMBRES	24 chambres avec vue sur l'océan
RESTAURATION	La spécialité de l'île sont les fruits de mer au gingembre, au citron vert et à l'ail : crabes de palétuvier, homards d'eau douce, calmars, crevettes géantes et poissons de toutes sortes. Un menu Swahili est disponible
HISTOIRE	Ouvert en 1967, l'hôtel appartient toujours à la même famille, qui le gère
LES « PLUS »	Être à deux degrés de l'équateur

A heaven here on earth...
Ngorongoro Crater Lodge, Ngorongoro Conservation Area

A heaven here on earth

Stand on the edge of the most impressive crater
on earth and look down. Far below you is all that is left of
what was once a great volcano. Three million years ago,
when the giant mountain collapsed, it formed a deep and
perfectly shaped basin. Steep walls ring the huge caldera
of Ngorongoro.

Within there is a remarkable assortment of wildlife, like
Noah's Ark in its selection. And perched on stilts on the rim
of the crater is an exceptional place to stay for the human
species that visit here. From the outside, the Ngorongoro
Crater Lodge looks like a Maasai village. One built on the
best possible site. Each suite has stunning views of the crater.
But from the inside, you could picture yourself to be in Paris.
The interior has a grandeur that is in accord with the dramatic
landscape that can be seen from the windows. Outside is
a real African Eden, teeming with thousands of animals.
Black rhinos, elephants, lions, leopards, buffaloes, and cheetahs roam free and wild, all around the renowned safari
lodge. Maasai warriors accompany you to and from your
room at night, making sure that you are out of harm's way.
Here, great wilderness and luxury are placed side by side.
Book to pack: "The African Queen" by Cecil Scott Forester

Ngorongoro Crater Lodge
Ngorongoro Conservation Area
Tanzania
Tel: + 255 (27) 11 809 43 14
E-mail: info@ccafrica.eu; safaris@ccafrica.com
Website: www.ngorongorocrater.com
www.great-escapes-hotels.com

DIRECTIONS	Ngorongoro Crater Lodge is accessible by scheduled flight from Arusha Airport, followed by a 2.5-hour road transfer
RATES	$$$
ROOMS	3 adjacent camps with 30 Maasai-inspired suites
FOOD	Pan-African
HISTORY	Built in 1997
X-FACTOR	The location, the decoration and diverse inhabitants

Ein Himmel hier auf Erden

Stehen Sie an der Kante des atemberaubendsten Kraters der
Welt und blicken Sie in die Tiefe hinab. Weit, weit unter Ihnen
liegt all das, was davon übrig ist, was einst ein großer Vulkan
gewesen ist. Vor drei Millionen Jahren brach der gigantische
Berg in sich zusammen und schuf dabei ein tiefes und perfekt
geformtes Becken. Steile Hänge bilden den kreisförmigen
Kraterkessel von Ngorongoro.

Und in ihm lebt eine unglaubliche Anzahl wilder Tiere, so
vielfältig in ihrer Art, wie einst auf Noahs Arche. Und auf
Stelzen gebaut, oben am Kraterrand befindet sich ein ganz
außergewöhnlicher Ort, an dem Besucher der menschlichen
Spezies verweilen können: Von außen sieht die Ngorongoro
Crater Lodge wie ein Massai Dorf aus – eines, das an der
denkbar besten Stelle errichtet wurde. Doch betrachtet man
sie von innen, so könnte man sich glatt vorstellen, man sei in
Paris. Die Pracht der Inneneinrichtung steht im Einklang mit
der dramatisch schönen Landschaft, die sich einem beim
Blick durch die Fenster eröffnet.

Draußen liegt ein wahrer afrikanischer Garten Eden, in welchem sich Tausende von Tieren tummeln: Schwarze Nashörner, Elefanten, Löwen, Leoparden, Büffel und Geparden
streifen wild und frei in der Nähe der renommierten Safari
Lodge umher. Abends begleiten Sie Massai Krieger zu Ihrer
Hütte und stellen sicher, dass Ihnen auch nichts passiert.
Großartige Wildnis und Luxus gehen hier Hand in Hand
miteinander einher.

Buchtipp: »Die African Queen« von Cecil Scott Forester

Le paradis sur terre

Approchez-vous du bord du cratère le plus impressionnant
du monde et penchez-vous. Tout en bas, vous apercevez tout
ce qui reste de ce qui fut un jour un immense volcan. Il y
a trois millions d'années, la montagne gigantesque qui se
dressait à cet endroit s'est effondrée et a laissé la place à
une cuvette profonde de forme parfaite entourée de parois
abruptes : l'énorme caldeira du Ngorongoro.

À l'intérieur vit une faune dont la remarquable diversité
n'est pas sans rappeler l'Arche de Noé. Au bord du cratère,
perché sur des pilotis, un refuge extraordinaire attend les
visiteurs. Vu de l'extérieur, Ngorongoro Crater Lodge a tout
d'un village massaï, un village érigé sur le meilleur site qui
soit. Chaque suite offre en effet une vue sensationnelle sur
le cratère. Toutefois, une fois à l'intérieur, on pourrait se
croire dans l'un des hôtels les plus chics de Paris étant don-
née l'harmonie entre la splendeur du décor et le spectaculaire paysage que l'on peut apercevoir à travers les fenêtres.
Ce dernier est un véritable éden peuplé de milliers d'animaux : rhinocéros noirs, éléphants, lions, léopards, buffles
et guépards sillonnent en toute liberté les alentours de cet
hôtel célèbre pour ses safaris. La nuit venue, les guerriers
massaï veillent sur votre sécurité en vous accompagnant
dans vos allées et venues hors de votre chambre.

Ici, les grandes étendues sauvages et le luxe se côtoient.

Livre à emporter : « Aventure africaine » de Cecil Scott Forester

ANREISE	Die Ngorongoro Crater Lodge kann per Flugzeug vom Flughafen Arusha und einem anschließenden 2,5-stündigen Autotransfer erreicht werden
PREIS	$$$
ZIMMER	3 nebeneinander liegende Camps mit 30 Suiten im Stil der Massai-Hütten
KÜCHE	Panafrikanisch
GESCHICHTE	Erbaut im Jahre 1997
X-FAKTOR	Die Lage, die Ausstattung und diverse Bewohner

ACCÈS	On accède à Ngorongoro Crater Lodge par vol régulier depuis l'aéroport d'Arusha, suivi d'un transfert en voiture de 2H30
PRIX	$$$
CHAMBRES	3 camps contigus avec 30 suites d'inspiration massaï
RESTAURATION	Panafricaine
HISTOIRE	Construit en 1997
LES « PLUS »	Le cadre, la décoration et les divers habitants du lieu

Baobab bungalows...
Tarangire Treetops, Tarangire Conservation Area

Baobab bungalows

The baobab tree is one of the most stunning sights in Africa. It can grow to a massive size; some are hundreds of years old. In many parts of the continent it is thought to be sacred. Legend has it that the tree so angered the gods that they tore it up then flung it back to earth, upside down, so it landed with its roots in the air.

The chalets that make up Tarangire Treetops Lodge are built on platforms high up in the canopy of these extraordinary trees. When we were children many of us fell in love with tree houses; sometimes we fell head over heels out of them. We had to give them up when we grew up. The 'huts' here are far more sophisticated than our childish kind; they may be in trees but that is where the resemblance ends – and all for the better. These are definitely a step up, and more.

A bar is set among the eaves of a massive baobab, where drinks are served before dinner. Even the dining 'room' is in a tree. And the creators of the Lodge really 'branched out' in their design of the chalets; each has a living room as well as a large bedroom. Of course a deluxe bathroom is part of this more adult version. The décor is stylish too, a skilful mix of local fabrics, Maasai craftsmanship and Swahili opulence. Down at ground level are the neighbours. Leopard, cheetah, lion, greater kudu and huge herds of elephant are at home here.

Book to pack: "The Flame Trees of Thika: Memories of an African Childhood" by Elspeth Huxley

Tarangire Treetops
Tarangire Conservation Area
Tanzania
Tel: + 255 (24) 223 21 19
Fax: + 255 (24) 223 21 19
E-mail: info@tanzania-adventure.com
Website: www.tanzania-adventure.com
www.great-escapes-hotels.com

DIRECTIONS	120 km/75 m south west of Arusha, or by plane to the Tarangire airstrip, 32 km/20 m away
RATES	$$
ROOMS	28 chalets built on top giant Baobab and Maroela trees
FOOD	Old world cuisine simmered in the African melting pot
HISTORY	The lodge was built with the local Maasai community. For every guest $20 is contributed to the village improvement
X-FACTOR	A chance to re-live childhood days

Baobab Bungalows

Der Affenbrotbaum gehört zu den verblüffendsten Sehenswürdigkeiten Afrikas. Er kann zu einer enormen Größe
heranwachsen und manche Exemplare sind mehrere hundert
Jahre alt. In vielen Teilen des Kontinents gilt der Baobab
als heilig. Eine Legende besagt, dass der Baum die Götter
so sehr ärgerte, dass sie ihn zerfetzten und ihn mit der
Krone nach unten zurück auf die Erde warfen, so dass
er mit den Wurzeln nach oben landete.

Die Hütten aus denen sich Tarangire Lodge zusammensetzt,
wurden auf Plattformen gebaut, die hoch oben auf diesen
Bäumen thronten. Kopfüber haben sich viele von uns als Kin-
der in die Idee verliebt, ein Baumhaus zu haben, kopfüber
ist so mancher hinuntergefallen, und als wir älter wurden,
mussten wir sie aufgeben. Diese Hütten hier sind von tech-
nisch viel raffinierterer Art, als es unsere »kindlichen«
Baumhäuser waren. Zwar befinden sie sich auf Bäumen,
doch damit endet die Ähnlichkeit auch schon, denn sie
sind definitiv viel ausgeklügelter. Wer möchte, kann vor dem
Abendessen einen Drink an der Bar einnehmen, die zwischen
die Stämme eines riesigen Affenbrotbaumes gebaut wurde.
Selbst der »Speisesaal« ist auf einem Baum gelegen. Und
was die Inneneinrichtung der Hütten angeht, kann man nur
sagen, dass die Gestalter der Lodge »astrein« geplant haben.
Jede Hütte hat sowohl ein Wohnzimmer, als auch ein Schlaf-
zimmer. Selbstverständlich sind auch Luxusbadezimmer Teil
dieser Erwachsenenversion eines Baumhauses. Der Dekor ist
ebenfalls stilvoll – eine gekonnte Mischung aus einheimischen Materialien, Massai-Handwerkskunst und opulenter
Swahili-Kunst.

Unten am Grund leben die Nachbarn. Hier sind Leopard,
Gepard, Löwe, die große Kuduantilope und riesige Elefantenherden zu Hause.

**Buchtipp: »Die Flammenbäume von Thika. Erinnerungen an
eine Kindheit in Afrika« von Elspeth Huxley**

Baobab bungalows

Le baobab est l'un des arbres les plus fascinants d'Afrique.
Considéré comme sacré dans de nombreuses régions du
continent, il peut atteindre des hauteurs vertigineuses et
certains spécimens sont plusieurs fois centenaires. La
légende dit que son aspect vient de ce que les dieux, cour-
roucés par son gigantisme, le déracinèrent et le renvoyèrent
sur terre, tête en bas et racines en l'air.

Les bungalows de Tarangire Treetops Lodge sont érigés sur
des plates-formes installées dans la voûte de ces arbres extra-
ordinaires. Enfants, nombre d'entre nous étaient friands des
cabanes construites dans les arbres. Certains même les trou-
vaient si bien qu'ils en tombaient parfois à la renverse. En
grandissant, nous avons dû y renoncer. Les « cabanes » de
Tarangire Treetops sont bien plus sophistiquées que celles
de notre enfance. Elles sont installées dans les arbres, soit,
mais la ressemblance s'arrête là, ce qui est tout à votre avantage. Ces cabanes sont d'une catégorie bien supérieure.

Un bar installé entre les feuilles d'un énorme baobab vous
attend pour un apéritif avant le dîner et même la salle du
restaurant est perchée dans un arbre. Par ailleurs, les créa-
teurs de l'hôtel ont exploré une branche réellement originale
de la conception de bungalows. En effet, chacun de ces der-
niers se compose d'un salon et d'une grande chambre, et
bien sûr, cette version adulte de la cabane est équipée d'une
salle de bain luxueuse. La décoration, tout aussi élégante,
est une habile combinaison d'étoffes locales, d'artisanat
massaï et d'opulence swahili.

Les voisins habitent au rez-de-chaussée : léopards, guépards,
lions, grands kudus et énormes troupeaux d'éléphants sont
ici chez eux.

Livre à emporter : « Le lion » de Joseph Kessel

ANREISE	Mit dem Auto 120 km südwestlich von Arusha; mit dem Flugzeug zum 32 km entfernten Flugplatz in Tarangire
PREIS	$$
ZIMMER	28 Hütten, die hoch oben in riesigen Affenbrot- und Maroelabäumen errichtet wurden
KÜCHE	Europäische Küche mit afrikanischem Einschlag
GESCHICHTE	Die Lodge wurde zusammen mit den einheimischen Massai gebaut. Pro Gast fließen 20 US$ in ein Hilfsprojekt
X-FAKTOR	Lassen Sie sich in ihre Kindheit zurückversetzen

ACCÈS	En voiture, à 120 km au sud-ouest d'Arusha, ou par avion jusqu'à Tarangire, distant de 32 km
PRIX	$$
CHAMBRES	28 bungalows construits en haut de baobabs et de maroelas géants
RESTAURATION	Cuisine européenne aux saveurs africaines
HISTOIRE	Hôtel construit avec les Massaï. Pour chaque résident, 20 $ sont investis dans l'aide à la population locale
LES « PLUS »	L'occasion de redevenir enfant

Spiritual therapy...
Mnemba Island Lodge, near Zanzibar

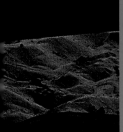

Mnemba Island Lodge, near Zanzibar

Spiritual therapy

If you had spent a week creating heaven and earth, this would be the place to rest on the seventh day. You could reflect on your work, and pat yourself on the back for creating such an idyllic place.

A few days at Mnemba Lodge, on a heart-shaped atoll off the coast of Zanzibar, is sure therapy for the spirit. This is one of the islands that are home to fragrant spices like nutmeg, cloves and cinnamon. Their stimulating scent, the sound of soft sea breezes rustling through the fronds of coconut palms and the lush plant life, all combine to make this an especially tempting place. Famed as being one of the most romantic spots in the world, Mnemba is a totally private island. Set in the turquoise Indian Ocean and surrounded by coral reefs, its pure white sand beaches are swathed around it like a halo. As suits an earthly paradise, it has a climate that is nearly perfect. Life is centred on the beach. Dinner is often served seated under the stars, at the edge of the water, with the guests' bare feet in the sea.

So, when you are feeling stressed enough to try the patience of a saint, this is the place to retreat to. A cloud nine is at hand.

Book to pack: "How I found Livingstone" by Henry Morton Stanley

Mnemba Island Lodge
P.O. Box 2055
Zanzibar
Tanzania
Tel: + 27 (11) 809 43 00
Fax: + 27 (11) 809 44 00
E-mail: webenquiries@ccafrica.com;
info@ccafrica.eu
Website: www.mnemba-island.com
www.great-escapes-hotels.com

DIRECTIONS	Mnemba lies 2 km/1.2 m north-east of the island of Zanzibar, a 20-minute cruise in a traditional boat
RATES	$$$$
ROOMS	10 secluded bungalows for up to 20 guests
FOOD	Pan-African cuisine with Mediterranean and Moroccan influences
X-FACTOR	Tropical paradise

Balsam für die Seele

Hätten Sie eine Woche damit zugebracht, Himmel und Erde zu erschaffen, so wäre dies der Ort, um am siebten Tage zu ruhen. Hier könnten Sie über Ihr Werk nachsinnen und sich selbst dafür auf die Schulter klopfen, dass Sie einen solch idyllischen Ort geschaffen haben.

Ein paar Tage in der Mnemba Lodge auf einem herzförmigen Atoll vor der Küste Sansibars zu verbringen ist sicherer Balsam für die Seele. Dies ist eine jener Inseln, die nach Muskat, Gewürzelken und Zimt riechen. Jener anregende Duft und das leichte Rascheln, wenn eine sanfte Meeresbrise zart durch die Wedel der Kokospalmen streicht, machen diese Insel zusammen mit der üppigen Vegetation zu einem besonders verführerischen Ort. Mnemba, dafür bekannt einer der romantischsten Flecken der Erde zu sein, ist eine vollkommen private Insel im türkisfarbenen Indischen Ozean, umgeben von Korallenriffen und gesäumt von weißen Sandstränden, wie von einem Heiligenschein. Wie es sich für das Paradies auf Erden gehört, weist die Insel zudem ein beinahe perfektes Klima auf. Das Leben spielt sich am Strand ab, und das Abendessen wird oftmals direkt am Strand unter dem Sternenhimmel serviert, während das Wasser die Füße sanft umspült.

Sollten Sie sich also gestresst genug fühlen, es einmal mit Engelsgeduld zu versuchen, so ist dies der Ort, an den Sie sich zurückziehen sollten. Wolke Sieben ist noch frei.

Buchtipp: »Wie ich Livingstone fand« von Henry Morton Stanley

Ressourcer l'âme et l'esprit

Si vous aviez passé une semaine à créer le ciel et la terre, c'est ici que vous vous reposeriez le septième jour. Vous pourriez alors méditer sur le travail accompli et vous féliciter d'avoir donné vie à un lieu aussi idyllique.

Quelques jours au Mnemba Lodge, situé sur un atoll en forme de cœur au large de la côte de Zanzibar, est la meilleure des thérapies de l'âme. Cette île est l'une de celles qui produisent des épices odorantes telles que la noix de muscade, le clou de girofle et la cannelle. Leur parfum stimulant et le souffle de la douce brise de mer qui fait bruisser les feuilles des cocotiers et la végétation exubérante en font un lieu particulièrement attrayant. Tenue pour l'un des endroits les plus romantiques au monde, Mnemba est une île où l'intimité est complète. Située au milieu de l'Océan Indien couleur turquoise, elle est entourée de barrières de corail et ses plages de pur sable blanc l'enveloppent tel un halo. Comme il se doit dans ce paradis terrestre, le climat est proche de la perfection. La vie s'organise autour de la plage : il vous arrivera souvent de dîner sous les étoiles, au bord de l'océan, les pieds dans l'eau.

Si votre stress est tel que vous ne savez plus à quel saint vous vouer, venez vous réfugier sur cette île. Le septième ciel vous attend.

Livre à emporter : « Comment j'ai retrouvé Livingstone » d'Henry Morton Stanley

ANREISE	Mnemba liegt 2 km nordöstlich der Insel Sansibar, eine 20-minütige Fahrt in einem traditionellen Boot	ACCÈS	Mnemba se trouve à 2 km au nord-est de Zanzibar, soit un trajet de 20 minutes à bord d'une embarcation traditionnelle
PREIS	$$$$	PRIX	$$$$
ZIMMER	10 abgeschiedene Bungalows für maximal 20 Gäste	CHAMBRES	10 bungalows isolés. Le nombre d'hôtes est limité à 20
KÜCHE	Panafrikanische Küche mit mediterraner und marokkanischer Note	RESTAURATION	Cuisine panafricaine aux influences méditerranéennes et marocaines
X-FAKTOR	Tropisches Paradies	LES « PLUS »	Un paradis dans les tropiques

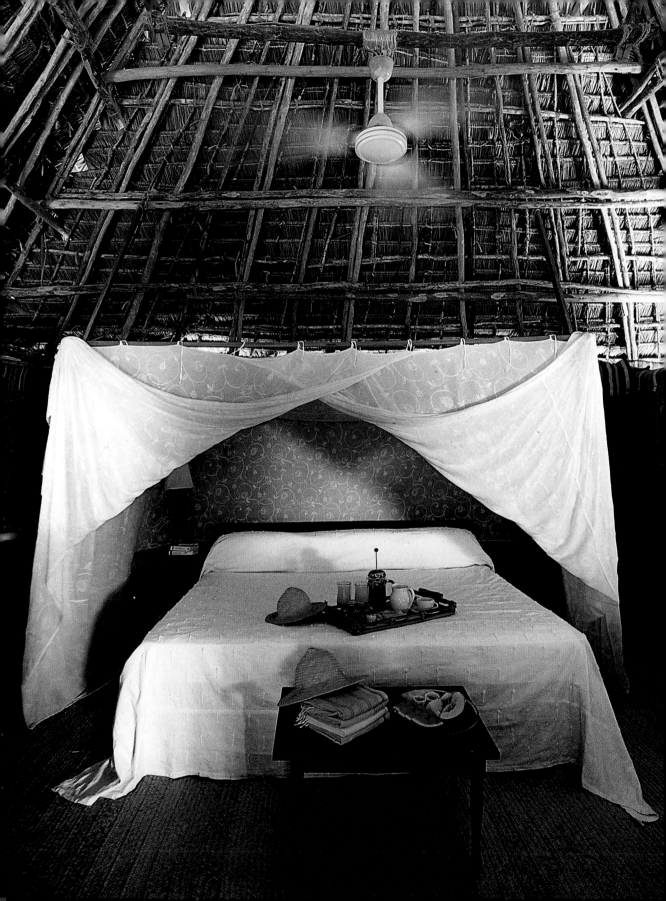

Spice of life...
Emerson & Green Hotel, Zanzibar

Emerson & Green Hotel, Zanzibar

Spice of life

When the Sultan of Oman came to visit this island, he was
so smitten by it that he at once moved here to live. That
was more than a century ago, but this is still an addictive
place. And its name is one of the most captivating.
Standing tall in the heart of Zanzibar's Stone Town is the
Emerson & Green Hotel. It was the residence of one of
the richest men in the Swahili Empire, who, due to his close
ties to the Sultan of the time, was allowed to build his house
as the second highest in the town, the highest being the
Sultan's own palace. From the hotel roof, the view stretches
over mosque minarets, Hindu temples, and church spires
to the ocean beyond. The narrow, crooked streets below are
lined with whitewashed houses, famous for their intricately
carved doors. A stroll through the colourful market, artisans'
workshops, mosques, an historic fort and sultans' palaces
makes for vibrant sights, and sounds.
And exotic aromas carried by the sea breeze scent the air.
Zanzibar was once the world's main source of cloves, and
in the fragrant spice gardens, most of the known tropical
spices, from cardamom to vanilla, can be seen growing in
their natural state.
**Book to pack: "Memoirs of an Arabian Princess from Zanzibar"
by Emily Ruete**

Emerson & Green Hotel
236 Hurumzi Street
P.O. Box 3417
Zanzibar, Tanzania
Tel: + 255 (77) 742 32 66
Fax: + 255 (77) 742 92 66
E-mail: 236hurumzibookings@zanlink.com
Website: www.emerson-green.com
www.great-escapes-hotels.com

DIRECTIONS	A short drive from Zanzibar airport
RATES	$$
ROOMS	10 double rooms
FOOD	Roof top restaurant serves up stunning views and sumptuous Arabian food
HISTORY	Built in the 19th century, it was restored to its former glory in the manner of a hotel in 1994
X-FACTOR	Opulent interior and exotic exterior

Die Würze des Lebens

Als der Sultan von Oman einst gekommen war, um diese Insel zu besuchen, war er gleich so von ihr hingerissen, dass er sofort zurückkehrte, um hier zu leben. Das ist nun mehr als hundert Jahre her, doch auch heute noch ist diese Insel ein Ort, der einen nicht mehr loslässt. Schon ihr Name ist so verheißungsvoll wie bei wenigen anderen.

Stolz ragt das Emerson & Green Hotel im Herzen von Stone Town in Sansibar in den Himmel. Einst war es der Wohnsitz eines der reichsten Männer im Königreich der Swahili. Da er eng mit dem damaligen Sultan befreundet war, gewährte man ihm das Recht, das zweithöchste Haus in der Stadt zu erbauen; das höchste Haus war der Palast des Sultans selbst. Vom Dach des Hotels schweift der Blick über Minarette und Moscheen, hinduistische Tempel und Kirchturmspitzen bis zum dahinter-liegenden Meer. Weiß getünchte Häuser, berühmt für ihre aufwändig geschnitzten Türen reihen sich aneinander und säumen die engen, verwinkelten Straßen. Ein Spaziergang über den Markt, vorbei an Kunsthandwerkstätten, Moscheen, einer historischen Festung und Sultanspalästen bringt lebhafte visuelle und akustische Eindrücke mit sich.

Und die Luft ist voll vom Duft exotischer Aromen, welche die Meeresbrise herbeiträgt. Sansibar war einst der weltweit bedeutendste Anbauort für Gewürznelken und in den duften-den Gewürzgärten kann man die meisten bekannten tropi-schen Gewürze, wie Kardamom oder Vanille, wild wachsen sehen.

Buchtipp: »Leben im Sultanspalast. Memoiren aus dem 19. Jahrhundert« von Emily Ruete

L'île aux épices

En visite sur l'île de Zanzibar, le sultan d'Oman en tomba amoureux et décida de s'y installer sur-le-champ. Bien que cette anecdote remonte à plus d'un siècle, l'île n'a rien perdu de son charme envoûtant et son nom reste synonyme de fascination.

L'hôtel Emerson & Green, qui s'élève en plein cœur de Stone Town, la ville de pierre de Zanzibar, était la résidence de l'un des hommes les plus riches de l'empire swahili. En raison de ses liens étroits avec le sultan de l'époque, il fut autorisé à construire la maison la plus haute de la cité après le palais du sultan. La vue du toit de l'hôtel vous dévoile des minarets de mosquées, des temples hindous et des flèches d'églises et s'étend jusqu'à l'océan. Les rues étroites et tortueuses en contrebas sont bordées de maisons blan-chies à la chaux, célèbres pour leurs portes d'entrée aux gravures complexes. Une visite au marché pittoresque, aux ateliers des artisans, aux mosquées, au fort historique et aux palais des sultans, et vous voilà transporté dans un univers plein de couleurs et de sons.

Des effluves exotiques transportés par la brise de mer embaument l'atmosphère : Zanzibar était jadis le principal producteur de clous de girofle et, dans ses jardins d'épices odorants, la plupart des épices tropicales connues, de la cardamome à la vanille, poussent à l'état naturel.

Livre à emporter : « Mémoires d'une princesse arabe » d'Emily Ruete

ANREISE	Kurze Fahrt vom Flughafen Sansibar
PREIS	$$
ZIMMER	10 Doppelzimmer
KÜCHE	Das Dachterrassenrestaurant bietet eine überwältigende Aussicht und aufwändige arabische Speisen
GESCHICHTE	Ursprünglich erbaut im 19. Jahrhundert wurde es im Jahre 1994 zum Hotel umgestaltet und erstrahlt nun in seiner alten Pracht
X-FAKTOR	Opulente Innenausstattung und exotische Umgebung

ACCÈS	À quelques minutes de l'aéroport de Zanzibar en voiture
PRIX	$$
CHAMBRES	10 chambres doubles
RESTAURATION	Le restaurant situé sur le toit de l'hôtel offre une vue exceptionnelle et propose des mets arabes exquis
HISTOIRE	Construit au XIXe siècle, le bâtiment a retrouvé sa splendeur passée en devenant hôtel en 1994
LES « PLUS »	Intérieur somptueux et environnement exotique

Sunset terrace...
Zanzibar Serena Inn, Zanzibar

Sunset terrace

This place has long been one of the world's busiest intersections. For centuries, the island has been a virtual crossroads; traffic from all corners of the globe has passed by here. Traders of spices or slaves, travellers from one land to others, all have left their mark on Zanzibar.

The architecture is one proof of that: much of the island's heritage is marked out in its buildings. Many of them have been given a new purpose. The Zanzibar Serena Inn is one of those. Two old houses on the seafront of historic Stone Town have been combined and restored to their earlier grandeur to form the hotel. Inside the design refers to the island's rich Arabian influences as well as its African lineage. It makes the most of its grandstand view of the Indian Ocean, too. The terrace is the prime place to see the stunning sunsets that light up the water as far as the mainland. The hotel offers day trips to its own private beach; a tranquil scene that is close to the infamous "slave caves" used for illegal slave trading after it was abolished. By the mid-19th century, Zanzibar was the world's largest producer of cloves, and it had the largest slaving centre on the east coast. Some fifty thousand slaves were put up for sale in its market each year. Few, if any, saw this place again

Book to pack: "Trade Wind" by Mary Margaret Kaye

Zanzibar Serena Inn
Kelele Square
Stone Town
Zanzibar, Tanzania
Tel: + 255 (24) 223 10 15
Fax: + 255 (24) 223 30 19
E-mail: serena@slh.com
Website: www.slh.com/serena
www.great-escapes-hotels.com

DIRECTIONS	Daily flights from Nairobi or Mombasa. Daily high speed ferries from Dar es Salaam c. 1.5 hours. On the sea front of the historic Stone Town on the western side of Zanzibar Island
RATES	$$$
ROOMS	47 double rooms, 4 suites
FOOD	Local seafood a speciality; the menu reflects the many cultural influences that have passed this way
HISTORY	Opened in 1997
X-FACTOR	Prime sea front position

Ein Platz an der Sonne

Lange Zeit stellte dieser Ort einen der wichtigsten Verkehrsknotenpunkte der Welt dar. Diese Insel war gewissermaßen über Jahrhunderte hinweg eine Art Kreuzung, durch welche der Verkehr aus allen erdenklichen Ecken der Erde floss. Gewürz- und Sklavenhändler, Weltreisende, alle haben sie ihre Spuren in Sansibar hinterlassen.

Ein Beweis dafür liegt nicht zuletzt in der Architektur, ein Großteil des kulturellen Erbes der Insel manifestiert sich sichtbar in den Gebäuden. Viele von ihnen erfüllen heute einen neuen Zweck. Dies ist auch der Fall beim Zanzibar Serena Inn: Zwei alte, direkt am Meer gelegene Häuser der historischen Stadt Stone Town wurden miteinander zu diesem Hotel zusammengeschlossen und erstrahlen, frisch renoviert, nun in ihrem altem Glanz. Die Innenausstattung bezieht sich deutlich auf die arabischen Einflüsse sowie die afrikanische Abstammung, welche die Insel so nachhaltig geprägt haben. Den bühnenartigen Ausblick auf den Indischen Ozean hätte sich das Hotel nicht besser zu Nutze machen können. Die Terrasse ist ein optimaler Ort, um die atemberaubenden Sonnenuntergänge zu beobachten, die das Wasser bis zum Festland hin aufleuchten lassen. Das Hotel bietet Tagestouren zu seinem Privatstrand an, einem ruhigen Schauplatz, nahe bei den berüchtigten Sklavenhöhlen, die nach Abschaffung der Sklaverei zum illegalen Sklavenhandel genutzt wurden. In der Mitte des 19. Jahrhunderts war Sansibar weltweit führend im Gewürznelkenanbau und galt außerdem als der größte Sklavenmarktplatz an der Ostküste. Jedes Jahr wurden hier etwa 50.000 Sklaven verkauft. Nur wenige, wenn überhaupt irgendeiner von ihnen, sah diesen Ort je wieder.

Buchtipp: »Tod in Sansibar« von Mary Margaret Kaye

La terrasse aux mille couchers de soleil

Cet endroit a longtemps été l'un des lieux de passge les plus fréquentés de la planète. Pendant des siècles, l'île fut un véritable carrefour où se croisaient des gens venus des quatre coins du monde. Marchands d'épices et d'esclaves, voyageurs, tous ont laissé une marque de leur passage à Zanzibar.

L'architecture en est une preuve puisqu'une grande partie du patrimoine de l'île se manifeste dans ses bâtiments. Nombre d'entre eux servent aujourd'hui de nouveaux objectifs. Ainsi, l'hôtel Zanzibar Serena Inn est formé par la réunion de deux vieilles maisons du front de mer de Stone Town, la ville de pierre historique, auxquelles on a rendu leur splendeur passée. À l'intérieur, le décor témoigne des riches influences arabes de l'île et de son lignage africain. Zanzibar Serena Inn a également su tirer le meilleur parti d'une vue incomparable sur l'Océan Indien. Sa terrasse est l'emplacement rêvé pour assister aux couchers de soleil époustouflants qui illuminent la mer jusqu'au continent. L'hôtel vous propose de passer la journée sur sa plage privée, lieu paisible situé à proximité des « grottes aux esclaves », tristement célèbres pour le commerce illégal des esclaves qui s'y tenait après l'abolition. Au milieu du XIXe siècle, Zanzibar était le premier producteur de clous de girofle au monde et abritait le plus grand marché d'esclaves de la côte est. Chaque année, quelque cinquante mille personnes y étaient mises en vente. Rares furent celles qui revirent un jour ce lieu.

Livre à emporter : « Zanzibar » de Mary Margaret Kaye

ANREISE	Mit dem Flugzeug (täglich) von Nairobi oder Mombasa. Oder ca. 1,5-stündige Fahrt mit dem Schnellboot (täglich) von Dar es Salaam. Das Hotel liegt an der dem Meer zugewandten Seite des historischen Stone Town
PREIS	$$$
ZIMMER	47 Doppelzimmer, 4 Suiten
KÜCHE	Fisch und Meeresfrüchte aus der Gegend. In der Speisekarte spiegeln sich die verschiedenen Einflüsse diverser Kulturen wider
GESCHICHTE	Eröffnet im Jahre 1997
X-FAKTOR	Direkt am Meer

ACCÈS	Vols quotidiens depuis Nairobi ou Mombasa. Traversées quotidiennes en ferry depuis Dar es Salaam d'environ 1H30. L'hôtel est situé sur le front de mer de Stone Town, la ville historique située à l'ouest de l'île de Zanzibar
PRIX	$$$
CHAMBRES	47 chambres doubles, 4 suites
RESTAURATION	Les fruits de mer de l'île sont la spécialité locale. Le menu reflète les nombreuses influences culturelles qui ont marqué l'île
HISTOIRE	Ouvert en 1997
LES « PLUS »	Front de mer incomparable

Barefoot luxury...
Chumbe Island Coral Park, Zanzibar

Chumbe Island Coral Park, Zanzibar

Barefoot luxury

Rising up on a small island between Zanzibar and Dar es Salaam is a lighthouse. Its flashing beam guides the dhows, boats that have crossed this sea for a thousand years. The tower also signals the location of one of the most spectacular coral gardens on earth. Beneath the water, corals in a kaleidoscope of colours teem with fish. Chumbe Island Coral Park is a private nature reserve, covered by an evergreen forest. This is an ecological sanctuary where the rare duiker antelope roam and giant coconut crabs climb to the top of trees in search of food. Few other buildings, or people, are here. Soaring thatched roofs amongst the foliage mark the existence of just seven bungalows. Water and energy are provided by nature, and they have solar-powered lights and hot water. All face the turquoise-blue ocean, and it takes just a few seconds to stroll to the beach and reef. Or you can just look at it, lying in your comfortable hammock.

This is rather like camping out, but in comparative luxury, and sleeping, dreaming, under a palm thatched roof.

Book to pack: "Robinson Crusoe" by Daniel Defoe

Chumbe Island Coral Park
P.O. Box 3203
Zanzibar
Tanzania
Tel: + 255 (24) 223 10 40
Fax: + 255 (24) 223 10 40
E-mail: ask@chumbeisland.com
Website: www.chumbeisland.com
www.great-escapes-hotels.com

DIRECTIONS	Fly to Zanzibar, take a boat from the beach at the Mbweni Ruins hotel
RATES	$$
ROOMS	7 bungalows
FOOD	Zanzibarian, Arabic, Indian and African cuisine
HISTORY	The Government of Zanzibar declared it a closed forest in 1994, and the management was entrusted to the Chumbe Island Coral Park
X-FACTOR	Castaway in style

Der Luxus, barfuß zu laufen

Auf einer kleinen Insel zwischen Sansibar und Dar es Salaam steht ein Leuchtturm. Sein blinkender Lichtstrahl weist den Dhows die Richtung, Booten, die schon seit tausend Jahren durch dieses Meer segeln.

Der Leuchtturm weist auch den Weg zu einem der eindrucksvollsten Korallenriffe der Welt. In den Tiefen des Meeres kann man hier inmitten der bunten Farbenpracht der Korallen ganze Schwärme von Fischen bewundern.

Chumbe Island Coral Park ist ein privater Naturschutzpark, der von einem immergrünen Wald überzogen ist, ein ökologisches Heiligtum, in dem die seltene Duiker Antilope frei umherstreift und Riesenkokosnusskrabben bei ihrer Nahrungssuche in die Baumkronen hinaufklettern. Sonst gibt es hier wenig andere Gebäude oder Menschen. An den strohgedeckten Dächern die aus den Blättern ragen, lässt sich erkennen, dass es hier nicht mehr als sieben Bungalows gibt. Wasser und Strom liefert die Natur, die Bungalows haben solarbetriebenes Licht und heißes Wasser und sind alle auf das türkisblaue Meer hinaus ausgerichtet. Mit nur wenigen Schritten gelangt man an den Strand und das Riff. Oder man genießt einfach nur deren Anblick, während man in seiner bequemen Hängematte liegt.

Das ganze erinnert eher an Camping, aber mit vergleichsweise hohem Luxus; schlafen und träumen unterm Palmendach.

Buchtipp: »Robinson Crusoe« von Daniel Defoe

Les pieds nus dans le luxe

Sur une petite île entre Zanzibar et Dar es Salaam se dresse un phare. Son faisceau lumineux guide les boutres, des bateaux qui traversent l'océan depuis un millier d'années. Cette tour indique également la présence de l'un des jardins de corail les plus spectaculaires du monde. Sous l'eau, les coraux et leur kaléidoscope de couleurs foisonnent de poissons. Chumbe Island Coral Park est une réserve naturelle privée recouverte d'une forêt à feuillage persistant. Dans ce sanctuaire écologique, les céphalophes, antilopes rares, s'ébattent en toute liberté et les crabes géants de cocotier grimpent au sommet des arbres à la recherche de nourriture. Il n'y a guère d'autres constructions, et la solitude règne. Des toits hauts et couverts de chaume dépassant du feuillage marquent la présence de sept bungalows seulement. L'eau est fournie par la nature et chauffée grâce à l'énergie solaire qui assure également l'éclairage. Tous les bungalows donnent sur l'océan bleu turquoise, et la plage et les récifs ne sont qu'à quelques secondes à pied. Bien sûr, vous pouvez aussi vous contenter de les observer de loin, confortablement installé dans votre hamac.

Vous aurez l'impression de camper, mais dans un camping de luxe, et vous dormirez et rêverez sous un toit recouvert de palmes.

Livre à emporter : « Robinson Crusoé » de Daniel Defoe

ANREISE	Fliegen Sie nach Sansibar, vom Strand des Mbweni Ruins Hotel aus nehmen Sie ein Boot
PREIS	$$
ZIMMER	7 Bungalows
KÜCHE	Inseltypische Gerichte, arabische, indische und afrikanische Küche
GESCHICHTE	Im Jahre 1994 wurde der Wald von der Regierung Sansibars unter Naturschutz gestellt und Chumbe Island Coral Park die Verwaltung übertragen
X-FAKTOR	Romantische Einsamkeit

ACCÈS	Après un vol jusqu'à Zanzibar, le bateau se prend sur la plage de l'hôtel Mbweni Ruins.
PRIX	$$
CHAMBRES	7 bungalows
RESTAURATION	Cuisine arabe, indienne, africaine et typique de Zanzibar
HISTOIRE	La forêt de l'île a été décrétée forêt protégée par le gouvernement de Zanzibar en 1994, et sa gestion a été confiée au Chumbe Island Coral Park
LES « PLUS »	Isolement et style

Treasure trove...

Frégate Island Private, Frégate Island

Frégate Island Private,
Frégate Island

Treasure trove

Long ago, pirates came in search of the treasure they
thought was to be found here. They were looking for gold
on this remote island, but their spades struck only rock.
The real treasure was not buried, but clearly able to be seen,
in the rich green landscape and hoard of bird-life. High on
the cliffs, hidden amongst cashew and almond trees, is some
more fortune: the villas of Frégate Island Resort. Each villa
is set apart, and blends into its lush background.
The spectacular sea views, secluded beaches, and coral reef
protected waters are just some of the spoils for those who
are privileged to stay here.
Privacy is one more of the riches here. Giant tortoises might
cross your path in this elite hideaway, but you will see few
people. Even fewer sightings will be made of the world's
rarest bird, the magpie robin. But you may hear its song,
one thought so beautiful that the bird was sought for a life
of captivity in gilded cages. Now it has found refuge on one
of the most unspoiled places on earth.
A safe haven that it shares, with others who seek to turn
their backs on the outside world for a while.
Book to pack: "Treasure Island" by Robert Louis Stevenson

Frégate Island Private
Frégate Island
Tel: + 27 (21) 556 99 84
Fax: + 27 (88) 021 556 99 84
E-mail: reservations@fregate.com
Website: www.fregate.com
www.great-escapes-hotels.com

DIRECTIONS	A 20 minute flight from the international airport at Mahé by a private chartered aircraft
RATES	$$$$
ROOMS	16 villas
FOOD	Gourmet, much of it grown on the island
X-FACTOR	Seclusion and luxury faraway in exotic surroundings

Eine Schatzinsel

Vor langer Zeit kamen Piraten hierher, um den Schatz zu heben, den sie hier vermuteten. Es war Gold, wonach sie auf dieser abgelegenen Insel suchten, doch ihre Spaten stießen nur auf Felsgestein.

Der wahre Schatz der Insel lag nirgendwo vergraben, sondern deutlich sichtbar in der üppigen grünen Landschaft und dem Reichtum der Vogelwelt. Hoch oben auf den Klippen verbirgt sich eine weitere Kostbarkeit: die Villen des Frégate Island Resort. Jede der Villen steht für sich allein und fügt sich harmonisch in den sattgrünen Hintergrund ein. Der Meeresblick, die Strände und die geschützten Korallenriffgewässer sind nur einige der Annehmlichkeiten, die sich jenen bieten, die das Glück haben hier verweilen zu dürfen. Ein weiterer Reichtum der Insel ist die Ungestörtheit, die man hier genießt. Und während einem an diesem exklusiven Zufluchtsort durchaus einige Riesenschildkröten begegnen können, trifft man Menschen hier eher selten. Noch weniger oft wird es einem gelingen, einen Blick auf die Seychellen-Schamadrossel zu erhaschen, den seltensten Vogel der Welt. Doch man kann sie singen hören und ihr Gesang galt lange Zeit als so betörend schön, dass diese Vögel gejagt wurden, um ihr Leben in goldenen Käfigen gefangen zu fristen. Heute haben sie einen geschützten Zufluchtsort in einem der unberührtesten Flecken der Erde gefunden – ein sicherer Hafen, den sie mit anderen teilen, die sich danach sehnen, dem Rest der Welt für eine Weile den Rücken zuzukehren.

Buchtipp: »Die Schatzinsel« von Robert Louis Stevenson

L'île aux trésors

Il y a de cela bien longtemps, des pirates débarquèrent sur cette île isolée, pensant y trouver un trésor. À la recherche d'or, leurs pelles ne rencontrèrent que du roc.

Le véritable trésor, un luxuriant paysage verdoyant et une multitude d'oiseaux, n'était pas enfoui mais exposé à la vue de tous. Le sommet des falaises recèle d'autres joyaux, tapis à l'ombre des anacardiers et des amandiers : les villas de la station balnéaire de l'île Frégate. Chacune d'entre elles a un style unique et se fond dans un paysage exubérant.

Les vues spectaculaires sur la mer, les plages retirées et les eaux protégées par des barrières de corail ne sont que quelques exemples des trésors découverts par ceux qui ont le privilège de séjourner dans ce lieu.

L'intimité et la solitude font partie des grandes richesses de cette retraite fastueuse, où votre chemin croisera peut-être celui de tortues géantes, mais plus difficilement celui de l'oiseau le plus rare du monde, le merle dyal. Toutefois, vous aurez peut-être la chance d'entendre son chant, si merveilleux que cet oiseau fut longtemps chassé puis gardé en captivité dans une cage dorée. Il a aujourd'hui trouvé refuge dans l'un des endroits les mieux préservés de la Terre, un havre de paix qu'il partage avec ceux qui souhaitent pour un temps oublier le monde extérieur.

Livre à emporter : « L'Île au trésor » de Robert Louis Stevenson

ANREISE	20-minütiger Flug mit einer privaten Chartermaschine vom internationalen Flughafen in Mahé
PREIS	$$$$
ZIMMER	16 Villen
KÜCHE	Gourmet, viele der Zutaten stammen aus inseleigenem Anbau
X-FAKTOR	Abgeschiedenheit und Luxus, entfernt vom Rest der Welt in exotischer Umgebung

ACCÈS	À 20 minutes de l'aéroport international de Mahé en avion-charter privé
PRIX	$$$$
CHAMBRES	16 villas
RESTAURATION	Gastronomique, essentiellement élaborée à partir des produits locaux
LES « PLUS »	Cadre exotique et luxueux, à l'écart du reste du monde

Ocean bliss.
Le Prince Maurice, Mauritius

Ocean bliss

Like Oscar Wilde, Mark Twain had a great deal to say on
most topics. And he seems to have journeyed to most continents; his writings pass judgement on where he had been.
His verdict on this place was that God had copied the idea
of heaven from Mauritius.

This could be taken to mean that it was created first, and
heaven was an afterthought. Whatever the right order might
be, it is true that this is one of the most naturally endowed
islands on earth. It has all the basics said to be ideal for an
island: white sands, aquamarine waters, palm trees and the
bluest of blue skies. But there is more to these essentials in
Mauritius. It has a style that comes from the influence of
quite a few different cultures. A mélange of African and
French, plus Muslim Chinese and Hindu traditions make
up the end product.

All this has been distilled to a stylish simplicity at Le Prince
Maurice Hotel. A perfect calm seems to have settled under
the soaring timber entrance vault. It is the gateway to a lush
'Garden of Eden' set between it and a private lagoon,
rimmed of course by a dazzling beach. There is an under-
stated glamour here, too, both in the surroundings and the
suites. Each of the suites has a colour theme that has been
inspired by the shades of spices, in a tribute to the condiments that have flavoured the island's history.

**Book to pack: "Following the Equator: A Journey Around the
World" by Mark Twain**

Le Prince Maurice		
Choisy Road	DIRECTIONS	On the north east coast of the island, 35 km/22 m east from the capital Port-Louis, 15 minutes from the International Airport SSR of Mauritius by helicopter
Poste de Flacq		
Mauritius	RATES	$$$
Tel: + 230 (402) 36 36	ROOMS	76 junior suites, 12 senior suites and 1 princely suite
Fax: + 230 (413) 91 29	FOOD	Aromatic and often spicy, from a range of restaurants, including one that floats on water
E-mail: info@princemaurice.com	HISTORY	Opened in 1998, named after Prince Maurice Van Nassau of Holland
Website: www.princemaurice.com		
www.great-escapes-hotels.com	X-FACTOR	A "Guerlain" spa, more bliss from the inspired creator of Shalimar

Perle im Ozean

Wie Oscar Wilde hatte auch Mark Twain zu den meisten
Dingen etwas zu erzählen und seinen literarischen Werken
entnehmen wir, dass er, die meisten Kontinente bereist hat.
Die Insel Mauritius erschien ihm als hätte sie Gott als
Vorlage für den Himmel gedient. Das würde allerdings
bedeuten, dass die Insel zuerst entstanden und der Himmel
ein nachträglicher Einfall sei.

Wie auch immer die Reihenfolge sein mag, es ist zweifellos
wahr, dass es kaum eine andere Insel auf der Welt gibt, die
so mit den Schönheiten der Natur gesegnet ist, wie diese.
Sie weist wirklich alle Eigenschaften einer idealen Trauminsel
auf: weiße Sandstrände, aquamarinblaues Wasser, Palmen und
einen strahlend blauen Himmel. Doch Mauritius bietet noch
weitaus mehr: Einflüsse verschiedenster Kulturen haben ihren
besonderen Stil geprägt, der aus einer Vermischung afrikanischer, französischer, sowie muslimischer, chinesischer und
hinduistischer Traditionen resultiert. Diese Elemente ver-
schmelzen im Le Prince Maurice Hotel zu einer stilvollen
Einfachheit. Unter dem hohen hölzernen Eingangsgewölbe
breitet sich eine wohl tuende Ruhe aus. Es ist das Tor zu
einem üppigen Garten Eden, der zwischen dem Haus und
einer privaten Lagune liegt, die von einem wunderschönen
Strand umrahmt ist. Sowohl die Umgebung, als auch die
Räumlichkeiten haben etwas dezent Glamouröses an sich. Jede
der Suiten ist nach einem Farbthema dekoriert, in Anlehnung
an die Gewürze und Aromen, welche die Geschichte der Insel
bestimmen.

Buchtipps: »Reise durch die alte Welt« von Mark Twain
»Die Wellen von Mauritius« von Lindsey Collen

Félicité au bord de l'océan

Tout comme Oscar Wilde, Mark Twain avait beaucoup de
choses à dire sur la plupart des sujets. Il semble que l'écrivain ait séjourné sur la plupart des continents. Dans ses
écrits, il porte un jugement sur les endroits où il s'est rendu.
Son verdict en ce qui concerne l'île Maurice est que Dieu
s'en est inspiré pour créer le paradis, ce qui laisserait penser
que l'île a été créée en premier et que le paradis n'en est
qu'une copie.

Quoi qu'il en soit, il s'agit à n'en pas douter de l'une des
îles les plus paradisiaques de la planète. Elle réunit tous les
ingrédients de base que l'on considère généralement comme
formant l'essence de l'île idéale : sable blanc, eau oscillant
entre le bleu et le vert, palmiers et ciel d'un bleu pur. Mais
l'île Maurice, c'est bien plus que cela. Héritière d'un style
marqué par plusieurs cultures différentes, elle est un creuset
de traditions africaines, françaises, musulmanes, chinoises
et hindoues.

L'hôtel Prince Maurice, véritable concentré de simplicité
et d'élégance, témoigne de ces influences. Un calme parfait
règne sous sa haute voûte d'entrée en bois. À l'intérieur,
vous découvrez un « jardin d'Éden » luxuriant attenant à un
lagon privé, bordé cela va sans dire d'une plage d'une beauté
éblouissante. Un charme discret et raffiné émane tant du
paysage que des suites. La couleur de chacune de ces dernières s'inspire d'une nuance d'épice, en hommage aux
condiments qui ont pimenté l'histoire de l'île.

Livres à emporter : « Les jours Kaya » de Carl de Souza
« Les voyages des innocents » de Mark Twain

ANREISE	An der nordöstlichen Küste gelegen, 35 km östlich von der Hauptstadt Port-Louis entfernt; 15-minütiger Flug mit dem Hubschrauber von Mauritius internationalen Flughafen SSR
PREIS	$$$
ZIMMER	76 Standardsuiten. 12 Luxussuiten und 1 Fürstensuite
KÜCHE	Aromatisch und oft scharf; es gibt verschiedene Restaurants, darunter auch ein schwimmendes
GESCHICHTE	Eröffnet im Jahr 1998, benannt nach Prinz Maurice Van Nassau zu Holland, einem Vorreiter des Gewürzhandels im Indischen Ozean
X-FAKTOR	Ein »Guerlain«-Spa, Entspannung à la Shalimar

ACCÈS	Situé sur la côte, au nord-est de l'île, à 15 minutes en hélicoptère de l'aéroport international de l'île Maurice et à 35 km à l'est de la capitale Port-Louis
PRIX	$$$
CHAMBRES	76 chambres-salons, 12 suites doubles et 1 suite royale
RESTAURATION	Cuisine aux aromates, assez épicée
HISTOIRE	Ouvert en 1998, l'hôtel tire son nom du Prince Maurice de Nassau, maître de la Hollande et pionnier du commerce des épices dans l'Océan Indien
LES « PLUS »	Centre de mise en forme Guerlain, l'ivresse des sens par le créateur inspiré de Shalimar

Wilderness paradise...
Sausage Tree Camp, Lower Zambezi National Park

Sausage Tree Camp,
Lower Zambezi National Park

Wilderness paradise

There is such a thing as a sausage tree; meat eaters may be delighted to know this. Sadly, for fans of sausages, it is not a real source of these treats. It is linked just in name only, and so called because its seedpods look like huge salamis. On the banks of the Zambezi, under a large and shady specimen of this tree, a camp has been created. The large white tents of Sausage Tree Camp sit high along the riverbank. These are marquees for connoisseurs of canvas, and come with all the creature comforts. Spacious and cool, the tents are simple and stylish. Welcome breezes waft through. Mahogany and acacia trees join with the sausages to form a thick forest that surrounds the camp on three sides. The view is over the river and a field of reeds; channels dotted with water lilies and, at times, with heavier things like pods of hippos. In the distance blue tinged mountains seem to float on the horizon.

This remote and unspoiled park is Zambia's newest. Huge herds of buffalo, elephant, and hippo are found here, along with lion, leopard and cheetah. Elusive and prickly creatures such as porcupines and honey badgers are also seen. Over four hundred species of bird have been noted in the area; the cry of the widespread African fish eagle often cuts through the air. Perhaps it is a sign that the fishing is superb here – for tiger fish, bream and huge catfish.

Book to pack: "North of South: an African Journey" by Shiva Naipaul

Sausage Tree Camp
Lower Zambezi National Park
Zambia
Tel: + 260 (211) 845 204
E-mail: info@sausagecamp.com
Website: www.sausagetreecamp.com
www.great-escapes-hotels.com

DIRECTIONS	Access by light aircraft from Lusaka, Kariba, Mfuwe or Livingstone to Jeki airstrip, then a 45-minute game drive to camp. Road and boat transfer is also available from Lusaka or Kariba
RATES	$$$
ROOMS	6 tents
FOOD	Sometimes real sausages, always good
HISTORY	Opened in August 1996
X-FACTOR	River boating in a wilderness paradise

Paradiesische Wildnis

Es gibt tatsächlich einen sogenannten Würstchenbaum,
Fleischesser werden dies mit Freude zur Kenntnis nehmen.
Traurig für alle Wurstliebhaber ist, dass an diesen Bäumen
nicht wirklich solche Leckereien wachsen. Nur der Name
verweist auf sie. Der Baum wird deswegen so genannt,
weil seine Samenschoten aussehen wie riesige Salamis.
Am Ufer des Sambesi, unter einem großen und schatten-
spendenden Exemplar jener Art, hat man ein Camp errichtet.
Entlang des Ufers liegen die weißen Zelte des Sausage Tree
Camps – große Zelte für Kenner des feinen Segeltuches, die
jeden erdenklichen Luxus bieten. Die geräumigen und küh-
len Zelte sind einfach und stilvoll und ein angenehmer Luft-
hauch weht durch sie hindurch. Zusammen mit den Sausage
Trees bilden Mahagoni- und Akazienbäume einen dichten
Wald, der das Lager an drei Seiten umgibt. Der Ausblick geht
auf den Fluss und ein Schilfrohrfeld hinaus; man blickt auf
die Kanäle, die mit Wasserlilien und manchmal auch mit
etwas schwereren Lebewesen, wie Nilpferdherden, übersät
sind. Die in der Ferne gelegenen, bläulich gefärbten Berge
scheinen am Horizont entlang zu treiben.
Dieser abgeschiedene und unberührte Park ist der jüngste
in Zambia. Hier trifft man auf große Büffel-, Elefanten-,
und Nilpferdherden, aber auch auf Löwen, Leoparden und
Geparden.
Auch publikumsscheue und kratzbürstige Lebewesen, wie
das Stachelschwein oder den Honigdachs kann man hier
zu Gesicht bekommen. In der Gegend wird das Vorkommen
von mehr als 400 verschiedenen Vogelarten verzeichnet,
und oft durchschneidet der Schrei des weitverbreiteten afrikanischen Fischadlers die Luft. Dies ist womöglich ein
Anzeichen dafür, wie hervorragend man hier Tigerfische,
Brassen und Riesenkatzenwelse fischen kann.
**Buchtipp: »North of South: an African Journey« von Shiva
Naipaul**

Paradis sauvage

Il existe bel et bien un arbre à saucisses. Voilà une nouvelle
qui ravira les amateurs de charcuterie. Malheureusement
pour eux, cet arbre ne produit pas réellement ces douceurs
et n'a de saucisse que le nom, qu'il tire de ses cosses res-
semblant à d'énormes salamis.
C'est sur les rives du Zambèze, à l'ombre d'un très grand
spécimen d'arbre à saucisses, que le camp Sausage Tree
Camp a été construit. Les grandes tentes blanches installées
le long du fleuve sont équipées de tout le confort matériel
et enchanteront les connaisseurs. Spacieuses, fraîches, elles
sont simples et élégantes, et une brise bienvenue y circule
en permanence. Les acajous, les acacias et les arbres à saucisses forment une épaisse forêt qui borde le camp sur trois
côtés. Le côté ouvert donne sur le fleuve, sur un champ
de roseaux et sur des canaux parsemés de nénuphars qui
accueillent parfois des invités de poids, les hippopotames.
Au loin, les montagnes teintées d'azur semblent flotter sur
la ligne d'horizon.
Ce parc reculé et bien préservé est le plus récent du pays.
D'immenses troupeaux de buffles, d'éléphants et d'hippopotames, des lions, des léopards et des guépards ou encore
des créatures insaisissables et armées de piquants telles
que le porc-épic et le ratel y cohabitent. Plus de quatre cents
espèces d'oiseaux ont été répertoriées sur ce territoire, et le
cri du pygargue vocifère, un aigle pêcheur très courant en
Afrique, fend l'air à intervalles réguliers. C'est peut-être le
signe que la pêche est de premier choix. Vous trouverez ici
des poissons tigres, des brèmes et d'énormes poissons-chats.
**Livre à emporter : « Au nord du Sud : Un voyage africain »
de Shiva Naipaul**

ANREISE	Mit dem Kleinflugzeug von Lusaka, Kariba, Mfuwe oder Livingstone aus zum Flugplatz Jeki, mit anschließender 45-minütiger Safarifahrt zum Camp. Von Lusaka oder Kariba aus ist auch ein Transfer mit dem Wagen oder per Boot möglich
PREIS	$$$
ZIMMER	6 Zelte
KÜCHE	Manchmal gibt es echte Würstchen, immer gut!
GESCHICHTE	Eröffnet im August 1996
X-FAKTOR	Flussschifffahrt in paradiesischer Wildnis

ACCÈS	En avionnette depuis Lusaka, Kariba, Mfuwe ou Living-stone jusqu'à la piste d'atterrissage de Jeki, puis trans-fert en voiture jusqu'au camp (45 min) pendant lequel vous pourrez observer la faune. Possibilité de transfert en voiture et en bateau depuis Lusaka ou Kariba
PRIX	$$$
CHAMBRES	6 tentes
RESTAURATION	Cuisine de qualité. De vraies saucisses sont parfois au menu
HISTOIRE	Ouvert en août 1996
LES « PLUS »	Navigation sur le fleuve au cœur d'un paradis sauvage

Going with the flow...

Matetsi Water Lodge, Matetsi Safari Area

Matetsi Water Lodge, Matetsi Safari Area

Going with the flow

An old Swahili proverb warns that appearances may well be deceptive. "Nyumba njema si mlango"; a good house is not judged by its door.

The entrance is not deceptive here. At Matetsi Water Lodge, the vast teak doors swing wide open to reveal true inner style and the sight of one of Africa's great rivers. The mighty Zambesi flows by the camp; boats and canoes will carry you on it. The lodge design is a polished blend of textures and colours. And from the canopied bed or the plunge pool on the tree-sheltered deck, the views are superb.

This game reserve is part of a huge wildlife paradise that spans two countries. Up to fifty thousand elephants, 'nature's great masterpiece', roam it – the greatest mass anywhere on earth. Lion calls can often be heard at night. It's best not to answer them. You can hear as well as see that the bird life is teeming. The Zambezi is home to the largest and most dangerous of African reptiles, the Nile crocodile. Its mean appearance is real; it has earned its rank as a killer. Large mammals are part of its diet.

Hippo too are often seen and heard along the river's edge. The loudest noise in these parts though is the rumbling of the Victoria Falls, just a short distance away. "Mosi oa tunya, the smoke that thunders" is the local name for the stunning cascade. It is a sight so impressive that many deem it one of the top wonders of our world.

Books to pack: "Livingstone's River: A History of the Zambezi Expedition, 1858–1864" by George Martelli
"Don't Let's Go to the Dogs Tonight" by Alexandra Fuller
"Butterfly Burning" by Yvonne Vera

Matetsi Water Lodge
Matetsi Safari Area
Victoria Falls
Zimbabwe
Tel: + 27 (11) 78 23 410
Fax: + 27 (11) 78 23 410
E-mail: info@wildlifeafrica.co.za
Website: www.wildlifeafrica.co.za
www.great-escapes-hotels.com

DIRECTIONS	Matetsi Water Lodge is accessible by scheduled flights to Victoria Falls Airport, followed by a 45-minute road transfer
RATES	$$$
ROOMS	3 separate camps each with 6 suites
FOOD	Cooked by a chef named Comfort – comfort food!
HISTORY	Opened in 1996
X-FACTOR	Life on the river, and near the stunning Victoria Falls

Sich treiben lassen

Ein altes Swahili Sprichwort warnt vor dem trügerischen Schein: »Nyumba njema si mlango«, ein gutes Haus erkennt man nicht an seiner Türe. In diesem Fall ist der Eingang nicht trügerisch. Wenn in der Matetsi Water Lodge die breiten Teakholztüren aufschwingen, geben sie nicht nur den Blick auf ein stilvolles Interieur, sondern auch auf einen von Afrikas beeindruckenden Flüssen frei. Der mächtige Sambesi, den Sie mit Booten und Kanus befahren können, fließt direkt am Camp vorbei. Die Innengestaltung der Lodge ist eine ausgefeilte Zusammenstellung von Materialien und Farben. Und der Ausblick, den man vom Schlafsofa oder vom Tauchbecken aus genießen kann, das sich unter dem Schutz von Bäumen auf der Terrasse befindet, ist fantastisch.

Dieses Wildreservat gehört zu einem riesigen Naturschutzparadies, das sich über zwei Länder erstreckt. Hier leben bis zu 50 000 Elefanten – so viele wie nirgendwo sonst auf der Welt. Des Nachts hört man oft Löwen, denen man besser keine Beachtung schenkt. Die vielen Vögel kann man sowohl hören, als auch sehen. Ebenfalls im Sambesi beheimatet ist das größte und gefährlichste aller afrikanischen Reptilien, das Nilkrokodil. Sein bedrohliches Aussehen täuscht keineswegs, denn es hat sich einen Namen als Killer gemacht. Und auf seinem Speiseplan stehen auch große Säugetiere.

Entlang des Flusses kann man die Nilpferde hören und sehen. Das lauteste Geräusch in dieser Gegend ist jedoch das Donnern der Victoria Falls, die nur wenige Meilen entfernt sind. »Mosi oa tunya«, den donnernden Rauch, nennen die Einheimischen die atemberaubenden Wasserfälle. Ihr Anblick ist derart spektakulär, dass viele Leute sie zu den größten Weltwundern zählen.

Buchtipp: »Schmetterling in Flammen« von Yvonne Vera

Au fil de l'eau

Un vieux proverbe swahili dit que les apparences sont parfois trompeuses : « *Nyumba njema si mlango* », « on ne juge pas la qualité d'une maison à sa porte ».

La porte d'entrée de Matetsi Water Lodge, elle, n'a rien de trompeur : les énormes battants en teck s'ouvrent en grand sur un intérieur véritablement luxueux d'où l'on peut admirer l'un des plus grands fleuves d'Afrique, le formidable Zambèze, qui coule près du camp et sur lequel vous pourrez naviguer en bateau ou en canoë. Le design de l'hôtel est un mélange sophistiqué de textures et de couleurs. La vue est toujours superbe, que vous l'admiriez de votre lit à baldaquin ou depuis le bassin de la terrasse protégée par les arbres.

Cette réserve naturelle fait partie d'un vaste paradis pour les animaux qui s'étend sur deux pays. Cinquante mille éléphants, ce « grand chef-d'œuvre de la nature » et la plus grande espèce terrestre, le parcourent en tous sens. La nuit, le rugissement des lions se fait souvent entendre. Mieux vaut ne pas y répondre. Et il suffit d'ouvrir les yeux et les oreilles pour se rendre compte que les oiseaux sont ici extrêmement nombreux. Le Zambèze abrite également le plus gros et le plus dangereux des reptiles africains : le crocodile du Nil. Son apparence sanguinaire reflète la réalité. En effet, sa réputation de tueur n'est pas usurpée, et les gros mammifères figurent parfois à son menu.

Souvent, vous verrez et entendrez également les hippopotames le long des rives du fleuve. Toutefois, le bruit le plus imposant dans cette partie de la Zambie est le grondement des stupéfiantes Chutes Victoria toutes proches, que les autochtones appellent *Mosi oa tunya*, « la fumée qui tonne ». Le spectacle est tellement impressionnant que nombreux sont ceux qui les considèrent comme l'une des plus belles merveilles du monde.

Livre à emporter : « Larmes de pierre : Une enfance africaine » d'Alexandra Fuller

ANREISE	Anreise mit dem Linienflug zum Victoria Falls Flughafen mit anschließender 45-minütiger Autofahrt	ACCÈS	Un vol régulier jusqu'à l'aéroport Victoria Falls, suivi d'un transfert en voiture de 45 minutes
PREIS	$$$	PRIX	$$$
ZIMMER	3 einzelne Camps, jedes mit 6 Suiten	CHAMBRES	3 camps distincts, disposant chacun de 6 suites
KÜCHE	Die Gerichte werden zubereitet von einem Koch, der Comfort heißt – Komfort(abel) speisen!	RESTAURATION	Le chef cuisinier s'appelle Comfort, et les plats qu'il élabore font honneur à son nom !
GESCHICHTE	Eröffnet im Jahre 1996	HISTOIRE	Ouvert en 1996
X-FAKTOR	Leben am Fluss und in der Nähe der großartigen Victoria Wasserfälle	LES « PLUS »	La vie au bord du fleuve ; proximité des Victoria Falls, chutes d'eau époustouflantes

Delta dawn...
Jao Camp, Okavango Delta

Delta dawn

Most of the land of Botswana is a desert. Yet deep within this fierce aridity lies a wetland, one that obtains its water from rain that falls in central Africa; rain over a thousand kilometres away.

At full flood, the channels of the Okavango Delta are fringed with papyrus reeds, and lilies float on its tranquil lagoons. Moving through the waterways in a mokoro – a traditional canoe – is one of the best ways to see the wildlife that teems here. Propelled by boatmen, the canoes slide silently past scenes just waiting to be filmed. The lagoons are home to hippo and crocodile, and the pools of water act as a magnet for thousands of birds. In the midst of this harbour is an oasis, Jao Camp. Secluded under a thick canopy of ancient trees, the whole camp is raised on decks that lift it so that it appears to be floating above the lush palms below. Each of the stylish rooms has thatched roofs with canvas walls. From October to March, the waters of the Delta largely subside and vast plains come into view. This is the time when lions, cheetahs and leopards are more in evidence, on day and night drives.

Book to pack: "Henderson the Rain King" by Saul Bellow

Jao Camp

Okavango Delta

Botswana

Tel: + 27 (11) 807 18 00

Fax: + 27 (11) 807 21 00

E-mail: enquiry@wilderness.co.za

Website: www.wilderness-safaris.com

www.great-escapes-hotels.com

DIRECTIONS	Accessible by scheduled flights from Johannesburg to Maun or Kasane, followed by a 30-minute flight from Maun, or a 1.5-hour flight from Kasane and a short drive to the camp
RATES	$$$
ROOMS	8 double room tents, 1 family tent
FOOD	Gourmet cuisine
HISTORY	Built in the Jao Reserve, the second reserve in Botswana not to hunt
X-FACTOR	Water and land combined

Dämmerung im Delta

Zum Großteil besteht das Territorium von Botswana aus Wüste. Doch tief im Inneren dieser rauen Dürrelandschaft liegt ein Feuchtgebiet. Sein Wasser stammt aus Regenfällen, die tausende von Kilometern entfernt, in Zentralafrika, vom Himmel gefallen sind.

Bei vollem Wasserstand säumt Papyrusschilf die Ufer entlang der Wasserkanäle des Okavango Deltas und Lilien schaukeln auf den stillen Lagunen. Um die Fauna, die sich hier tummelt, zu beobachten, sollte man sich am besten mit einem Mokoro, einem traditionellen Kanu, auf den Wasserstrassen fortbewegen. Von Menschenhand angetrieben, gleiten diese Kanus geräuschlos an Schauplätzen vorbei, die nur darauf warten, gefilmt zu werden. Die Lagunen beheimaten Nilpferde und Krokodile und die Wasserbecken ziehen Tausende von Vögeln an wie ein Magnet. In der Mitte dieses Gebietes befindet sich eine Oase, das Jao Camp. Das gesamte Camp liegt abgeschirmt unter einem dichten Gewölbe uralter Baumkronen; es wurde auf Plattformen errichtet, wodurch es den Anschein erweckt, als würde es wie ein Floß über den dichten darunter liegenden Palmen dahintreiben. Jedes der stilvollen Zimmer hat ein strohgedecktes Dach und Segeltuchwände.

Von Oktober bis März versickert ein Großteil des Wassers und eröffnet den Blick auf weite Ebenen. In dieser Jahreszeit trifft man – bei Tagesausflügen oder nächtlichen Fahrten – häufiger auf Spuren von Löwen, Geparden und Leoparden.

Buchtipp: »Der Regenkönig« von Saul Bellow

Aube sur le delta

La plus grande partie du Botswana est désertique. Toutefois, au cœur de ce paysage aride et âpre, on trouve des étendues marécageuses. L'eau qui les alimente provient de la pluie qui tombe à plus de mille kilomètres de là, en Afrique centrale.

Au plus fort des crues, les canaux du delta d'Okavango sont bordés de papyrus, et des lis flottent sur ses lagunes paisibles. Pour se déplacer sur ces cours d'eau et observer la faune pullulante, rien de tel qu'un *mokoro*, pirogue traditionnelle que des bateliers font glisser silencieusement au milieu de paysages qui feraient rêver n'importe quel cinéaste. Les lagunes abritent hippopotames et crocodiles, et les plans d'eau agissent comme des aimants sur des milliers d'oiseaux. Là, au cœur de ce havre de paix, vous trouverez une oasis : Jao Camp. Protégé par une épaisse voûte formée par la frondaison d'arbres centenaires, le camp est construit sur pilotis et formé de pontons qui le surélèvent et donnent l'impression qu'il flotte sur les luxuriants palmiers en contrebas. Chacune des élégantes chambres présente un toit de chaume et des murs tapissés de toile.

D'octobre à mars, le niveau des eaux du Delta baisse considérablement et laisse la place à de vastes plaines. C'est à cette époque que vous avez le plus de chances d'apercevoir des lions, des guépards et des léopards lors d'excursions diurnes ou nocturnes.

Livre à emporter : « Le Faiseur de pluie » de Saul Bellow

ANREISE	Nur per Linienflug von Johannesburg nach Maun oder Kasane mit anschließendem 30-minütigen Flug von Maun, oder 1,5-stündigen Flug von Kasane und kurzer Autofahrt zum Camp erreichbar
PREIS	$$$
ZIMMER	8 Zelte für 2 Personen, 1 Familienzelt
KÜCHE	Für Feinschmecker
GESCHICHTE	Erbaut im Jao Reserve, dem zweiten Reservat in Botswana, in dem das Jagen verboten ist
X-FAKTOR	Die Kombination von Wasser und Land

ACCÈS	Accessible seulement par vols réguliers de Johannesburg à Maun ou à Kasane, suivi d'un vol de 30 minutes de Maun ou d'1H30 de Kasane et d'un court trajet de 10 minutes en voiture jusqu'au camp
PRIX	$$$
CHAMBRES	8 tentes-chambres doubles, 1 tente familiale
RESTAURATION	Cuisine gastronomique
HISTOIRE	Construit dans la réserve de Jao, la seconde réserve du Botswana où la chasse est interdite
LES « PLUS »	Alliance de l'eau et de la terre

Water world...
Nxabega Okavango Safari Camp, Okavango Delta

Water World

The money here is named after water, which seems a fitting choice in a country that is mostly dry. Its main unit is the pula, which means rain, and it is split into thebe – raindrops. It is a gentle prompt that this is a land, and a continent, where water is precious.

Water is not scarce in this part. Botswana is dry, but not here, in the Delta. 'On safari' in this wilderness of clear water and tall grass, at dawn or at dusk, can be a truly buoyant event. A trip in a mokoro, just gliding in slow motion through the maze of channels, is a memory to treasure. Papyrus reeds edge the waterways; silver flashes of fish break the surface; all sorts of creatures move in and across the grass; the air is warm and still. It will come back to mind when you are on a clogged motorway.

In the language of the "river bushmen", Nxabega means "place of the giraffe". The tents are on high legs too, raised wooden platforms.

African ebony and strangler fig trees give shade to the camp; its style is one of subtle class, and from your veranda or the main lodge, the view is spectacular. There are few people here in this landscape, but it is full of wildlife. Birds are everywhere in and on the water in the reeds and the trees on the ground and in the air. This is one of the few places in Africa where you can see the animals from the waterways; and they can see you.

Book to pack: "Rain Fall" by Barry Eisler

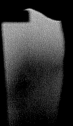

Nxabega ("neh-sha-bay-ga") Okavango
Safari Camp
Moremi Wildlife Reserve
Okavango Delta
Botswana
Tel: + 27 (11) 809 43 00
Fax: + 27 (11) 809 44 00
E-mail: safaris@ccafrica.com
Website: www.ccafrica.com
www.great-escapes-hotels.com

DIRECTIONS	Accessible only by scheduled flights from Johannesburg to Maun or Kasane, followed by a 30-minute flight from Maun, or a 1.5-hour flight from Kasane and a short drive to the camp
RATES	$$$
ROOMS	10 safari tents for up to 18 guests
FOOD	A fusion of local ingredients with African flavours
HISTORY	Opened in April 2000 under Conservation Corporation Africa (CC Africa)
X-FACTOR	The Delta itself, one of the most extraordinary wild places in Botswana

Wasserwelt

Die Bezeichnung für Geld leitet sich hier von der Bezeichnung für Wasser ab. Eine treffende Wortverwandtschaft, wenn man bedenkt, dass dies ein überwiegend trockenes Land ist. Die größere Einheit der hiesigen Währung heißt pula, was Regen bedeutet, und setzt sich aus den so genannten thebe, Regentropfen, zusammen – ein behutsamer Hinweis darauf, dass auf diesem Kontinent Wasser eine Kostbarkeit darstellt. In diesem Teil des Landes herrscht allerdings keine Wasserknappheit. Zwar ist Botswana sehr trocken, jedoch nicht hier im Delta. In der Morgen- oder Abenddämmerung kann man eine schwimmende Safaritour durch diese Wildnis aus klarem Wasser und hohem Gras machen. Eine solche Tour in einer Mokoro, bei der man langsam durch das Labyrinth von Kanälen gleitet, ist ein unvergessliches Erlebnis. Papyrus umsäumt die Wasserstraßen, silbern blitzen die Fische an der Wasseroberfläche, die verschiedensten Tiere bewegen sich im und über dem Gras, die Luft ist warm und ruhig. All diese Eindrücke werden plötzlich zu Ihnen zurückkommen, wenn Sie wieder einmal im Stau auf der Autobahn stehen.

In der Sprache der Flussbuschmänner bedeutet Nxabega »Ort der Giraffe«. Auch die Zelte haben hier lange Beine: Sie stehen auf hölzernen Plattformen. Afrikanisches Ebenholz und Würgefeigen spenden dem Camp, das in einem feinen, klassischen Stil gehalten ist, Schatten. Von der Veranda oder dem Hauptgebäude aus kann man eine spektakuläre Aussicht genießen. In dieser Gegend leben nur wenige Menschen, dafür umso mehr Tiere. Überall sind Vögel, in und auf dem Wasser, im Schilf und in den Bäumen, am Boden und in der Luft. Dieser Ort ist einer der wenigen in Afrika, von dem man die Tiere vom Wasser aus beobachten kann und sie uns.

Buchtipp: »Regenroman« von Karen Duve

Éclat aquatique

L'eau est à l'origine du nom de la monnaie botswanaise, ce qui est tout à fait approprié pour un pays où, dans l'ensemble, le climat est sec. L'unité monétaire de référence du pays est le *pula*, pluie, lui-même divisé en *thebe*, gouttes de pluie. Ceci montre à quel point l'eau est un bien précieux dans le pays et sur le continent. Contrairement à ce qui se passe dans le reste du pays, l'eau ne manque pas dans la région du delta. Partir en safari, à l'aube ou au crépuscule, dans cette vaste étendue sauvage couverte d'eau pure et de hautes herbes peut s'avérer une expérience extrêmement vivifiante. Vous chérirez longtemps le souvenir de votre excursion à bord d'un *mokoro* glissant au ralenti à travers un dédale de canaux : les papyrus bordant les voies navigables, l'éclair argenté des poissons rompant la surface de l'eau, les multiples créatures s'enfonçant dans l'herbe, l'air chaud et calme. Toutes ces images vous reviendront lorsque vous vous retrouverez coincé dans un embouteillage sur l'autoroute.

Dans la langue des « bushmen du fleuve », Nxabega signifie « maison de la girafe ». Les tentes du camp sont elles aussi dressées sur de « hautes jambes », ces pilotis qui soutiennent des plates-formes en bois surélevées.

Installé à l'ombre des ébéniers africains et des figuiers des Banyans, le camp est d'une élégance subtile et la vue depuis votre véranda ou le hall principal est spectaculaire. La solitude du lieu n'est troublée que par l'abondance de la faune : les oiseaux sont partout, dans et sur l'eau, au milieu des roseaux et perchés dans les arbres, sur le sol ou dans les airs. Le delta est l'une des rares régions africaines où vous pouvez apercevoir les oiseaux depuis les voies navigables et où eux aussi peuvent vous observer...

Livres à emporter : « La ville du désert et de l'eau » de Jean-François Ménard
« Déluge » de Karen Duve

ANREISE	Nur per Linienflug von Johannesburg nach Maun oder Kasane mit anschließendem 30-minütigen Flug von Maun, oder 1,5-stündigen Flug von Kasane und kurzer Autofahrt zum Camp erreichbar
PREIS	$$$
ZIMMER	10 Safarizelte für maximal 18 Gäste
KÜCHE	Verschmelzung einheimischer Zutaten mit einer Auswahl afrikanischer Aromen
GESCHICHTE	Unter der Leitung von CC Africa im April 2000 eröffnet
X-FAKTOR	Das Delta selbst! Es ist einer der außergewöhnlichsten Orte in der Wildnis und mit großer Wahrscheinlichkeit Botswanas wertvollste natürliche Ressource

ACCÈS	Uniquement par vol régulier jusqu'à Maun ou Kasane, puis vol de 30 minutes à partir de Maun ou d'1H30 à partir de Kasane en avionnette et court trajet en voiture
PRIX	$$$
CHAMBRES	10 tentes accueillant 18 personnes maximum
RESTAURATION	Grand choix et possibilité de savourer des plats aux saveurs africaines
HISTOIRE	Ouvert en avril 2000 sous la direction de Conservation Corporation Africa (CC Africa)
LES « PLUS »	Le delta lui-même, l'un des sites les plus extraordinaires du Botswana et l'une de ses ressources naturelles plus précieux encore que les diamants

Studying the tracks...
Sandibe Safari Lodge, Okavango Delta

Sandibe Safari Lodge, Okavango Delta

Studying the tracks

You never know when you might need a few basic skills. Here at Sandibe Lodge, you can apply yourself to gaining some.

Interpretive bush walks are in the care of a local San – Bushman – guide. This is your chance to learn traditional bush skills; like making rope from grasses, how to construct traps, light fires with friction sticks, and how to track animals. Or you can just sit and watch them.

Elephants have walked the meandering paths by the camp for hundreds of years. Perhaps moved by this, the lodge has been built with a commitment to "treading lightly on the earth." No trees were felled in its construction; instead, the cottages were built in a natural clearing. Their roofs are thatched, but that is where the resemblance to a usual cottage ends.

These are far removed from the sort that this English word often means. Their airy rooms are styled with a rich fusion of colour and texture, and of tactile fabrics like silk and leather, woven mats, copper and rough-hewn wood. An exotic landscape surrounds them, a forest of wild palms and twisting trees, flanked by channels of a delta that contains 95 per cent of all the surface water in Botswana. The mud spires of giant termite mounds and great baobab trees stand out in the scenery. Sandibe is set in a backwater, and all the better for it. A wealth of wildlife, birds, and plants thrive in the grass-wept floodplains of the Okavango Delta.

"The art of moving gently, without suddenness, is the first to be studied by the hunter, and more so by the hunter with the camera." Karen Blixen

Books to pack: "Among the Elephants" by Iain & Oria Douglas-Hamilton
"The White Bone" by Barbara Gowdy

Sandibe Safari Lodge
Adjacent to Moremi Wildlife Reserve
Okavango Delta
Botswana
Tel: + 27 (11) 809 43 00
Fax: + 27 (11) 809 44 00
E-mail: safaris@ccafrica.com
Website: www.sandibe.com,
www.ccafrica.com
www.great-escapes-hotels.com

DIRECTIONS	Accessible only by scheduled flights from Johannesburg to Maun or Kasane, followed by a 30-minute flight from Maun, or a 1.5-hour flight from Kasane and a short drive to the camp
RATES	$$$
ROOMS	8 double-room cottages
FOOD	Pan-African cuisine
HISTORY	Opened in 1998
X-FACTOR	Unique cottages in an idyllic environment

Auf Spurensuche

Man kann nie wissen, wann man einmal ein paar grundlegen-de Fertigkeiten gebrauchen kann. Hier, in der Sandibe Lodge, können Sie bei Kulturwanderungen durch die Buschlandschaft unter der Führung eines einheimischen San, eines Buschman-nes, einige davon erwerben.

Dies ist Ihre Chance, die Fertigkeiten zu erlernen, die ein Buschmann traditionellerweise beherrscht, zum Beispiel ein Seil aus Gräsern zu flechten, Fallen zu bauen, Feuer durch das Aneinanderreiben zweier Stöckchen zu entflammen und die Fährten der Tiere zu lesen. Oder aber Sie bleiben einfach sitzen und beobachten die Tiere nur. Seit Hunderten von Jah-ren schon ziehen die Elefanten entlang der Pfade, die sich am Camp vorbeischlängeln. Vielleicht war dies der ausschlagge-bende Grund, warum man sich beim Bau der Lodge dazu verpflichtet hat, sanft vorzugehen, es wurde kein Baum für ihre Errichtung gefällt. Stattdessen baute man die Hütten in eine natürliche Lichtung hinein. Ihre Dächer sind strohge-deckt, doch damit endet auch schon jedwede Ähnlichkeit mit einer gewöhnlichen Hütte. Die Hütten, von denen hier die Rede ist, sind weit entfernt von dem, was dieses Wort im Deutschen oft impliziert. Eine luxuriöse Verbindung von Far-ben und Materialien verleiht den luftigen Räumen Stil: sinnli-che Stoffe wie Seide und Leder, gewebte Matten und Kupfer kombiniert mit grob behauenem Holz. Umgeben sind die Hüt-ten von einer exotischen Landschaft, einem Wald aus wilden Palmen und gekrümmten Bäumen, an dem die Kanäle eines Flussdeltas vorbeilaufen, das 95 Prozent des gesamten Oberflä-chenwassers in Botswana enthält. Gegen den Horizont zeich-nen sich die Schlammspitzen der riesigen Termitenhügel und beeindruckende Affenbrotbäume ab. Ein großer Vorteil von Sandibe ist, dass es in einem Stauwasserbereich gelegen ist. Im Gras- und Schwemmland des Okavango Deltas tum-melt sich eine reiche Artenvielfalt von Tieren, Vögeln und Pflanzen.

Buchtipps: »Unter Elefanten« von Iain und Oria Douglas-Hamilton »Der weiße Knochen« von Barbara Gowdy

Repérer les empreintes

Qui sait si certaines techniques de survie ne vous seront pas un jour utiles ? Pour en apprendre quelques-unes, venez à Sandibe Lodge.

Un guide local *San*, un bushman, vous y attend pour vous entraîner dans des excursions explicatives à travers la brousse. Vous aurez la possibilité d'apprendre les techniques tradition-nelles de la brousse, notamment comment élaborer une corde avec de l'herbe, construire des pièges, faire démarrer un feu à l'aide de morceaux de bois et suivre la trace des animaux. Vous pourrez également vous contenter d'observer le guide. Les éléphants qui arpentent les chemins sinueux du camp depuis des centaines d'années sont peut-être à l'origine de l'engagement des constructeurs de l'hôtel, « fouler la terre d'un pas léger ». Aucun arbre n'a été abattu pour la construction de l'établissement et les chaumières ont été érigées dans une clairière naturelle. Leurs toits sont recou-verts de chaume, mais la ressemblance avec des chaumières traditionnelles s'arrête là.

Ces chaumières-là n'ont pratiquement rien à voir avec la définition habituelle du mot : les chambres, claires et spa-cieuses, présentent une riche association de couleurs et de textures, des étoffes qui invitent à la caresse, par exemple la soie et le cuir, des tapis tissés, du cuivre et du bois équarri. Un environnement exotique entoure les pavillons : une forêt de palmiers sauvages et d'arbres volubiles bordée des canaux d'un delta qui contient 95 % de la totalité de l'eau de surface du Botswana. Les flèches de boue des monticules des ter-mites géantes et les immenses baobabs tranchent sur le pay-sage. Sandibe est situé au cœur des eaux mortes, ce qui est tout à son avantage. Une profusion d'animaux sauvages, d'oiseaux et de plantes s'épanouit dans les plaines inon-dables du delta d'Okavango balayées par les herbes.

Livres à emporter : « Les éléphants et nous » de Iain et Oria Douglas-Hamilton « Un lien sûr » de Barbara Gowdy

ANREISE	Nur per Linienflug von Johannesburg nach Maun oder Kasane mit anschließendem 30-minütigen Flug von Maun, oder 1,5-stündigen Flug von Kasane und kurzer Autofahrt zum Camp erreichbar	ACCÈS	Accessible uniquement par vol régulier de Johannesburg à Maun ou à Kasane, suivi d'un vol de 30 minutes de Maun ou d'1H30 de Kasane et d'un court trajet en voiture jusqu'au camp
PREIS	$$$	PRIX	$$$
ZIMMER	8 Hütten für 2 Personen	CHAMBRES	8 pavillons pour 2 personnes
KÜCHE	Panafrikanisch	RESTAURATION	Cuisine pan-africaine
GESCHICHTE	Eröffnet im Jahre 1998	HISTOIRE	Ouvert en 1998
X-FAKTOR	Einzigartige Hütten in idyllischer Umgebung	LES « PLUS »	Des pavillons au style unique au cœur d'un cadre idyllique

Pavilions in the wild...
Mombo Camp, Okavango Delta

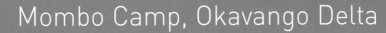

Pavilions in the wild

This is where the sound of cameras might just be louder than the noises of nature. On safari now, most of the wildlife is seen through a lens, rather than down the sights of a rifle.

Just who or what is the hunter here is pleasantly confused. Mombo Camp is most famous for the number of predators on show– the animal kind that is. Close to the camp is the home territory of many prides of lions, cheetahs, leopards and African painted wolves. The game viewing here is so good that this is where many documentary filmmakers and photographers choose to lie in wait for their quarry. As well as the great variety and mass of wildlife, the game reserve where Mombo is situated is endowed with a matchless diversity of landscape. Marshes and floodplains, acacia bushveld, grassland and mopane forests provide a habitat that suits and shelters many creatures.

The habitat on offer to humans is under canvas, in tents that are a far cry from the usual. These are more like luxury pavilions, each one raised off the ground by wooden decks, with great views across the Delta. The scene inside is also a very fine one.

Book to pack: "Dangerous Beauty. Life and death in Africa: True Stories from a Safari Guide" by Mark C. Ross

Mombo Camp	
Moremi Game Reserve	
Okavango Delta	
Botswana	
Tel: + 27 (11) 807 18 00	
Fax: + 27 (11) 807 21 00	
E-mail: enquiry@wilderness.co.za	
Website: www.wilderness-safaris.com	
www.great-escapes-hotels.com	

DIRECTIONS	Accessible only by scheduled flights from Johannesburg to Maun or Kasane, followed by a 30-minute flight from Maun, or a 1.5-hour flight from Kasane and a short drive to the camp
RATES	$$$$
ROOMS	12, in two independent camps, Mombo with 9 rooms and Little Mombo with 3
FOOD	Gourmet African and Western style
HISTORY	Mombo Lodge has been completely rebuilt and the new camps opened in June 2000
X-FACTOR	Prolific wildlife observed from a luxurious setting

Pavillons in der Wildnis

Hier ist das Klicken der Kameraauslöser teilweise lauter als die Geräusche der Natur selbst. Wer heute auf Safari geht, betrachtet die wilden Tiere eben eher durch die Linse einer Kamera, als durch das Zielfernrohr eines Gewehres.

Wer oder was der Jäger ist, scheint hier auf angenehme Weise vertauscht zu sein. Mombo Camp ist berühmt dafür, dass man eine Unmenge an wilden Raubtieren – und Raubtiere sind sie nun einmal – zu Gesicht bekommt. Nahe beim Camp liegt das Heimatgebiet von Löwen, Geparden, Leoparden und Steppenwölfen. Die Gegend eignet sich so hervorragend zur Wildbeobachtung, dass viele Dokumentarfilmer und Fotografen hierher kommen, um sich auf die Lauer zu legen. Das Wildreservat in welchem Mombo liegt, besticht jedoch nicht nur durch die großartige Vielfalt seiner Tierwelt, sondern ist auch mit einer beispiellos abwechslungsreichen Landschaft gesegnet. Marsch- und Schwemmland, Akazienwälder, Graslandschaften und Mopanewälder stellen für viele Tiere einen idealen Lebensraum dar.

Der unmittelbare Lebensraum der menschlichen Besucher liegt unter Segeltuchplanen, in Zelten, die alles andere als gewöhnlich sind. Sie erinnern vielmehr an Luxuspavillons; jedes Einzelne steht auf einem hölzernen Deck über dem Grund und bietet einen großartigen Ausblick über das Delta. Auch innen herrscht eine sehr gehobene Atmosphäre.

Buchtipp: »Afrika. Das letzte Abenteuer. Die Geschichte eines Safariführers« von Mark C. Ross

Pavillons sauvages

Ici, seul le crépitement des appareils photo est susceptible de couvrir les bruits de la nature. De nos jours, lors d'un safari, la plupart des animaux sont observés à travers un objectif plutôt qu'à travers la lunette d'un fusil.

Il est difficile en ces lieux de distinguer le chasseur du chassé, ce qui s'avère tout à fait plaisant. Mombo Camp est en partie célèbre pour son grand nombre de prédateurs. (Nous parlons bien sûr des animaux !) Nombreuses sont les troupes de lions, de guépards, de léopards et les meutes de chiens sauvages africains qui ont établi leur territoire à proximité du camp. L'endroit est tellement idéal pour l'observation des animaux que de nombreux réalisateurs de documentaires et photographes ont choisi ce site pour guetter leur proie. Outre sa faune extrêmement variée et abondante, la réserve naturelle qui accueille Mombo est dotée d'un paysage à la diversité incomparable. Les marécages et les plaines inondables, les steppes à acacia, les prairies et les forêts de mopani sont des habitats parfaitement adaptés aux multiples créatures qu'ils abritent.

L'habitat proposé aux visiteurs est fait de toile, mais les tentes qui les accueilleront n'ont rien à voir avec les tentes habituelles. Comparables à des pavillons de luxe, montées sur pilotis et pontons en bois, elles donnent sur les superbes paysages du delta. Et l'intérieur est tout aussi beau.

Livre à emporter : « Grands chasseurs sous la lune : Les lions du Savuti » de Beverly Joubert et Dereck Joubert

ANREISE	Nur per Linienflug von Johannesburg nach Maun oder Kasane mit anschließendem 30-minütigen Flug von Maun, oder 1,5-stündigen Flug von Kasane
PREIS	$$$$
ZIMMER	12, in zwei voneinander unabhängigen Camps, 9 Zimmer in Mombo und 3 in Little Mombo
KÜCHE	Afrikanische Feinkost und Westlicher Stil
GESCHICHTE	Mombo Camp und Little Mombo wurden neu aufgebaut und im Juni 2000 wurden die neuen Camps 800 m von der alten Stelle entfernt eröffnet
X-FAKTOR	Luxuriöse Ausstattung im Schoß von Mutter Natur

ACCÈS	Accessible uniquement par vol régulier de Johannesburg à Maun ou à Kasane, suivi d'un vol de 30 minutes de Maun ou d'1H30 de Kasane et d'un court trajet en voiture jusqu'au camp
PRIX	$$$$
CHAMBRES	12, situées dans deux camps séparés : Mombo (9 chambres) et Little Mombo (3 chambres)
RESTAURATION	Cuisine gastronomique africaine et occidentale
HISTOIRE	Mombo Camp et Little Mombo ont été entièrement reconstruits et de nouveaux camps ont ouvert en juin 2000 sur un nouveau site situé à 800 m de l'ancien
LES « PLUS »	Observation de la faune depuis un cadre luxueux

Where the buffalo roams...
Singita Boulders Lodge, Kruger National Park

Where the buffalo roams

In the heart of Africa, the search for prey is as old as time. As the sun starts to set and the heat of the day subsides, lions, leopards, cheetahs, hyenas and jackals begin to hunt. Whatever each of them outruns will be on their menu.

Of course your dinner will be served to you; unlike the animals, you are not required to hunt down your food.

At dusk, your personal game guard will escort you from your suite at the deluxe Boulders Lodge to the open-air boma, for pre-dinner drinks around a blazing fire. Seated here, you can gaze out over the vast plains inside the exclusive wildlife sanctuary of Singita.

For an animal watcher Singita is a dream come true. The park has a wealth of wildlife. The top five on the animal kingdom list, the elephant, lion, leopard, buffalo and rhinoceros are all here. From your private deck at this sumptuous lodge, you can watch hippos feeding nearby and cheetahs racing in the distance, and spot a giraffe moving gracefully past. Whether travelling by day in vehicles, on walking expeditions to get close to the smaller inhabitants of the bush, or on night safaris to view rare nocturnal creatures, there is much to observe.

Book to pack: "Disgrace" by J.M. Coetzee

Singita Boulders Lodge	
Sabi Sand Game Reserve	
Kruger National Park	
Mpumalanga Province	
South Africa	
Tel: + 27 (21) 68 33 424	
Fax: + 27 (21) 67 16 776	
E-mail: singita@singita.com	
Website: www.singita.com	
www.great-escapes-hotels.com	

DIRECTIONS	A 75-minute flight northeast from Johannesburg to Skukuza, approximately 5 hours driving time from Johannesburg to Singita
RATES	$$$$
ROOMS	9 double suites
FOOD	Traditional dishes and indigenous African venison specialities
HISTORY	Opened in December 1996
X-FACTOR	Panoramic wildlife views from a luxury vantage point

Im Königreich der Tiere

Das Jagen nach Beute ist im Herzen Afrikas so alt wie die Zeit selbst. Wenn die Sonne allmählich untergeht und die Hitze des Tages abklingt, begeben sich Löwen, Leoparden, Geparden, Hyänen und Schakale auf die Jagd. Was auch immer sie sich erhetzen, steht auf ihrem Speiseplan.

Im Gegensatz zu den Tieren müssen Sie nicht erst selbst auf die Jagd gehen. In der Abenddämmerung geleitet Sie Ihr persönlicher Wildwächter von Ihrer Suite in der luxuriösen Boulders Lodge zu der unter freiem Himmel gelegenen Boma, wo Sie, während Sie an einem lodernden Feuer sitzen, einen Aperitif einnehmen. Von hier kann man seinen Blick schweifen lassen über die weiten Ebenen, die innerhalb des Naturschutzparks von Singita liegen.

Für Tierbeobachter ist Singita ein wahr gewordener Traum. Der Park beheimatet eine Fülle von wild lebenden Tieren. Die fünf wohl imposantesten Mitglieder im Königreich der Tiere, der Elefant, der Löwe, der Leopard, der Büffel und das Nashorn – sie alle leben hier. Von Ihrer privaten Terrasse aus können Sie in dieser feudalen Unterkunft Nilpferde beim Fressen beobachten, Geparden zusehen, die in der Ferne jagen oder eine Giraffe entdecken, die anmutigen Schrittes vorüberzieht.

Ob auf Tagestouren mit dem Auto, bei Wanderexpeditionen, die einen näher an die kleineren Buschbewohner herankommen lassen, oder auf nächtlichen Safaris, bei denen man seltene Nachtwesen erspähen kann – es gibt viel zu beobachten.

Buchtipp: »Schande« von J.M Coetzee

Sur les traces du buffle

En Afrique, la chasse remonte à la nuit des temps.

Au crépuscule, lorsque la chaleur décroît, lions, léopards, guépards, hyènes et chacals commencent à traquer leur proie, et tout ce qui tombe sous leurs griffes figure à leur menu.

Quant à vous, ne vous inquiétez pas. À la différence des animaux, vous n'aurez pas à chasser pour manger à votre faim. Au crépuscule, vous quitterez votre suite du luxueux Boulders Lodge escorté par votre garde-chasse personnel et rejoindrez le boma à l'air libre pour un apéritif autour d'un grand feu. Vous pourrez alors contempler les vastes plaines de l'exceptionnelle réserve d'animaux sauvages de Singita. Avec sa faune abondante, le parc de Singita est un rêve devenu réalité pour les amateurs d'animaux. Les cinq espèces les plus emblématiques du règne animal, à savoir l'éléphant, le lion, le léopard, le buffle et le rhinocéros, sont toutes représentées. Depuis votre terrasse privée, vous verrez les hippopotames se nourrir à proximité, les guépards filer comme le vent dans le lointain et les girafes cheminer gracieusement aux abords de cet hôtel somptueux. Que vous partiez de jour, en voiture ou à pied, à la découverte des autres animaux de la brousse ou que vous observiez des créatures nocturnes rares lors d'un safari de nuit, vous aurez beaucoup à voir.

Livre à emporter : « Disgrâce » de J.M. Coetzee

ANREISE	75-minütiger Flug nordöstlich von Johannesburg nach Szukuza, mit dem Auto etwa 5-stündige Fahrt von Johannesburg nach Singita (500 km)	
PREIS	$$$$	
ZIMMER	9 Suiten für je zwei Personen	
KÜCHE	Traditionelle Gerichte und einheimische, afrikanische Wildspezialitäten	
GESCHICHTE	Eröffnet im Dezember 1996	
X-FAKTOR	Luxuriöser Aussichtspunkt mit Wildpark Panorama	

ACCÈS	75 minutes de vol, direction nord-est, de Johannesburg à Skukuza. En voiture, à environ 5 heures de Johannesburg (500 km)
PRIX	$$$$
CHAMBRES	9 suites pour deux personnes
RESTAURATION	Plats traditionnels et spécialités indigènes de venaison africaine
HISTOIRE	Ouvert en décembre 1996
LES « PLUS »	Point de vue luxueux permettant d'admirer le panorama de la faune et de la flore

Earthly pleasures...
Sabi Sabi Earth Lodge, Skukuza

Earthly pleasures

If you feel that you are overly 'wired', this is a place where you can 're-earth' yourself.

You can go to ground, in both the factual and symbolic sense. But, save for the cost, there is nothing you must give up. No forfeit is needed. This is a cocoon of sheer luxury sculpted deep into the earth. The ultimate shelter, where you are insulated from the outside world, yet still open to it.

At first glance, this sumptuous lodge seems quite austere. Sabi Sabi Earth Lodge follows the contours of the landscape, so well that it is all but hidden. The buildings are kept low in the environment. Within the lodge, the colours echo the earth shades of the outside walls. It was built in an organic style with all natural resources, as far as was possible. The result is a quite distinctive place that makes a strong visual impact. Tree trunks have been creatively used; crafted as bars, benches, and just decorative forms. But the plain look is deceptive. There is a double standard of sorts at play here. Simple materials are used, but only the best has been chosen. Each suite is minimalist, yet it has its own butler, and pool. One has its own exercise room, steam room, study, and kitchen. There is a spa, a vast wine cellar, and a meditation garden.

Of course, Africa is the real star here. A vast bushveld panorama lies in wait; wild creatures are just a walk or drive away.

Books to pack: "Rare Earth" by Peter D. Ward and Donald Brownlee

"Letters from the Earth" by Mark Twain

Sabi Sabi Earth Lodge
Sabi Sand Private Game Reserve
South Africa
Tel: + 27 (13) 735 52 61
Fax: + 27 (13) 735 52 60
E-mail: earth@sabisabi.com
Website: www.sabisabi.com
www.great-escapes-hotels.com

DIRECTIONS	A 5-hour drive from Johannesburg, or a 2-hour scenic drive from Nelspruit; daily flights from Johannesburg International Airport to Skukuza Airport
RATES	$$$$
ROOMS	12 suites, 1 presidential suite
FOOD	Fusion of African, French and Italian cuisine
HISTORY	Sabi Sabi Earth Lodge was opened in 2001
X-FACTOR	The most stylish 'bunker' in existence

Irdische Vergnügen

Wenn Sie vollkommen abgespannt sein sollten und sozusagen knapp vor einem Kurzschluss stehen, so ist hier der
richtige Ort, um sich wieder zu »erden«. Hier kann man im
wörtlichen wie im übertragenen Sinn auf den Boden zurück-
kehren. Dabei müssen Sie jedoch auf nichts verzichten und
keinerlei Abstriche machen. Dies ist ein Kokon des puren
Luxus, der tief in die Erde hinein geformt wurde, ein ultima-
tiver Unterschlupf, in dem man von der Außenwelt
geschützt, aber dennoch nicht von ihr abgeschnitten ist.
Auf den ersten Blick erscheint diese opulente Lodge eher
asketisch. Sabi Sabi Earth Lodge passt sich den Konturen
der Landschaft so gut an, dass sie schwer zu erkennen ist.
Die Gebäude sind niedrig gehalten. In den Innenräumen der
Lodge werden die Erdschattierungen der Außenwände farb-
lich wieder aufgegriffen. Beim Bau hat man versucht, so viele
organische Baumaterialien zu verwenden wie nur irgend
möglich. Das Ergebnis dieser Bauweise ist ein ganz besonde-
rer Ort, der einen recht ungewöhnlichen Anblick bietet.
Baumstämme wurden auf kreative Art und Weise integriert
und funktionieren als Bar, Bänke oder dienen einfach dekorativen Zwecken. Doch das schlichte Erscheinungsbild trügt.
Zwar wurden einfache Materialien verarbeitet, doch nur qua-
litative hochwertige. Jede der Suiten wirkt minimalistisch,
hat aber einen eigenen Diener und einen Pool. Eine davon
verfügt über einen eigenen Trainingsraum, Dampfbad,
Arbeitszimmer und Küche. Außerdem gibt es ein Heilbad,
einen gut sortierten Weinkeller und einen Meditationsgarten.
Die eigentliche Sehenswürdigkeit ist auch hier natürlich
Afrika selbst und der herrliche Ausblick über die weite
Buschlandschaft. Wildtiere sind nur einen Fußmarsch oder
eine kurze Fahrt weit entfernt.
Buchtipps: »Unsere einsame Erde« von Peter D. Ward und
Donald Brownlee
»Briefe von der Erde« von Mark Twain

Plaisirs terrestres

Si vous vous sentez trop stressé, voici l'endroit idéal pour
vous ressourcer.
Il vous permettra de retourner à la terre, au sens propre
comme au sens figuré, sans devoir renoncer à quoi que ce
soit. Si ce n'est le coût de votre séjour, vous n'aurez pas à
en payer le prix. Sabi Sabi Earth Lodge est un cocon de luxe
absolu sculpté profondément dans la terre, l'abri suprême
où vous serez isolé du monde extérieur sans toutefois lui
tourner le dos.
À première vue, cet hôtel somptueux semble assez austère.
Sabi Sabi Earth Lodge épouse les contours du paysage ; si
bien d'ailleurs qu'il s'en trouve presque dissimulé. Ses bâtiments peu élevés ne déparent pas l'environnement. Les
couleurs de l'intérieur évoquent les nuances des murs exté-
rieurs qui sont de couleur terre. Pour la construction de
l'hôtel, de style organique, des matériaux entièrement natu-
rels ont été utilisés chaque fois que cela était possible.
Le résultat est un édifice original qui fait forte impression.
Les troncs d'arbre y sont utilisés de façon créative ; ils ont
en effet été travaillés pour devenir des bancs, des bars ou
tout simplement des formes décoratives. Mais l'apparence
simple et dépouillée de l'hôtel est trompeuse. Il existe ici
deux mesures. Les matériaux de construction sont basiques
mais de la plus haute qualité. Les suites sont minimalistes,
mais chacune a son propre majordome et sa piscine. L'une
d'elles compte même une salle de sport, un sauna, un
bureau et une cuisine. L'hôtel dispose également d'installa-
tions de cure thermale, d'une grande cave à vins et d'un
jardin de méditation.
Bien sûr, la véritable star reste l'Afrique : une vue panoramique sur la vaste steppe vous attend, et les animaux
sauvages ne sont qu'à quelques minutes de marche ou
de voiture.
Livre à emporter : « La plus belle histoire de la terre »
d'André Brahic et al.

ANREISE	Eine etwa 5-stündige Fahrt von Johannesburg oder 2-stündige Panoramafahrt von Nelspruit aus. Täglich Flüge von Johannesburg International Airport zum Skukuza Airport
PREIS	$$$$
ZIMMER	12 Suiten, 1 Präsidentensuite
KÜCHE	Mischung afrikanischer, französischer un italienischer Speisen
GESCHICHTE	Die Sabi Sabi Earth Lodge wurde im Jahre 2001 eröffnet
X-FAKTOR	Der stilvollste »Bunker« der Welt

ACCÈS	À 5 heures de Johannesburg en voiture ou à 2 heures de Nelspruit le long d'une route touristique. Vols quotidiens en partance de Johannesburg jusqu'à l'aéroport de Skukuza
PRIX	$$$$
CHAMBRES	12 suites, plus une suite présidentielle
RESTAURATION	Cuisine fusion africaine, française et italienne
HISTOIRE	Sabi Sabi Earth Lodge a ouvert ses portes en 2001
LES « PLUS »	Le « bunker » le plus élégant du monde

Safari for the soul..
Garonga Lodge, Limpopo Province

Garonga Lodge, Limpopo Province

Safari for the soul

Everyone needs to take a safari for the soul, some 'time out' to find inspiration and to restore lost vigour.

The tent camp of Garonga, with its billowy ceilings of cream coloured canvas is just the place for such a mission. The floors and walls are sculpted from clay. In this place your senses too can be shaped and soothed. The camp is the perfect place to relax and reflect. To ease your stress, special treatments are at hand in a secluded "sala" in the bush. Taking a long soak in the deep bath that is nestled in the bush is one of the most memorable experiences. Being in the midst of such natural splendor is invigorating in itself. A night spent sleeping in a tree house out in the superb landscape that surrounds the camp is another way to relax. You can even cast off your clothes. To make this easy, a "kikoi" – a style of sarong – is given to each guest. It is suggested that it be worn during one's stay, even to dinner at night.

The camp looks out over a riverbed, one that an elephant herd is drawn to visit. Watching from the terrace or pool, you can be sure that elephants will come out from the bushes and feed just a few metres away from you.

Book to pack: "West with the Night" by Beryl Markham

Garonga Lodge
P.O. Box 737
Hoedspruit 1380
Limpopo Province
South Africa
Tel: + 27 (87) 806 20 80
Fax: + 27 (87) 806 20 80
E-mail: reservations@garonga.com
Website: www.garonga.com
www.great-escapes-hotels.com

DIRECTIONS	Daily scheduled flights from Johannesburg to Phalaborwa and Hoedspruit. Transfers are available from airport to the camp
RATES	$$
ROOMS	6 double rooms, 1 luxury suite
FOOD	To feed the soul
HISTORY	Built in 1997
X-FACTOR	Taking a bush bath under the stars

Seelensafari

Jeder sollte einmal auf Seelensafari gehen, einmal eine
Art Auszeit nehmen, um neue Inspirationen zu erlangen
und verloren gegangene Vitalität wieder aufzufrischen.
Das Zeltcamp von Garonga mit seinen gewölbten Decken
aus crèmefarbenem Segeltuch ist genau das Richtige für
solch ein Vorhaben. Boden und Wände sind aus Lehm
geformt. Hier können auch die Sinne neu geformt und
verwöhnt werden. Das Camp ist der ideale Ort zum
Entspannen und Nachdenken. Wer Stress abbauen möchte,
kann sich spezielle Entspannungsbehandlungen in einer
abgelegenen »Sala« im Busch gönnen. Ein langes erholsa-
mes Bad tief verborgen in der Wildnis ist wohl eine der ein-
prägsamsten Erinnerungen, die Sie mitnehmen werden.
Sich inmitten solcher Naturschönheit zu befinden, ist an
sich schon wohl tuend. Eine Nacht in einem Baumhaus in
dieser fantastischen Landschaft zu verbringen, ist eine
wunderbare Methode, um neue Kräfte zu schöpfen. Selbst
Ihre Kleider können Sie hier abstreifen. Damit dies leichter
fällt, bekommt jeder Gast einen »Kikoi« – eine Art Sarong.
Es ist vorgesehen, dass er während des gesamten Aufent-
haltes, selbst beim Abendessen getragen wird.
Das Camp öffnet sich zu einem Flussbett hin, das von
Elefantenherden aufgesucht wird. Wenn Sie auf der
Terrasse oder am Bassin stehen, können Sie so gut wie
sicher sein, dass Elefanten aus dem Busch kommen und
nur einige Meter von Ihnen entfernt auf Nahrungsuche
gehen.
**Buchtipp: »Westwärts mit der Nacht. Mein Leben als Fliegerin
in Afrika« von Beryl Markham**

Un safari de l'âme

Tout le monde a besoin de reprendre des forces, de faire
une pause pour retrouver inspiration, énergie et vitalité.
Pour cela, rien de tel qu'un safari.
Le camp fixe de Garonga, avec ses tentes au plafond en toile
crème se gonflant et ondoyant sous le vent, est l'endroit le
mieux adapté à une telle entreprise. Tout comme les sols et
les murs sculptés dans l'argile, vos sens reprendront forme
et s'apaiseront. Le camp est le lieu idéal pour se détendre
et réfléchir : pour calmer votre stress, des soins spéciaux
vous sont proposés dans un « sala » retiré situé en pleine
brousse. Un long bain dans les vastes bassins à l'air libre est
une expérience inoubliable, et la nature alentour est en elle-
même revigorante. Vous pouvez également vous détendre
en passant une nuit dans une cabane perchée dans un arbre,
au milieu du superbe paysage qui entoure le camp. Vous
pouvez même oublier vos vêtements. En effet, chaque hôte
se voit remettre un « kikoi » (sarong), que nous vous suggé-
rons de porter pendant votre séjour, même au moment du
dîner.
Le camp donne sur le lit d'un fleuve près duquel vous apercevrez peut-être un troupeau d'éléphants. Si vous observez
le paysage depuis la terrasse ou la piscine, vous les verrez
sortir des buissons et se nourrir à seulement quelques
mètres de vous.
**Livre à emporter : « Vers l'ouest avec la nuit » de Beryl
Markham**

ANREISE	Tägliche Linienflüge von Johannesburg nach Phalaborwa und Hoedspruit. Transfer vom Flughafen zum Camp möglich
PREIS	$$
ZIMMER	6 Doppelzimmer und 1 Luxussuite
KÜCHE	Zum Seele verwöhnen
GESCHICHTE	Im Jahre 1997 erbaut
X-FAKTOR	Ein Bad im Busch unter Sternenhimmel

ACCÈS	Vols quotidiens en partance de Johannesburg jusqu'à Phalaborwa et Hoedspruit. Possibilité de transfert de l'aéroport jusqu'au camp
PRIX	$$
CHAMBRES	6 chambres doubles et 1 suite de luxe
RESTAURATION	Réconfortante et savoureuse
HISTOIRE	Construit en 1997
LES « PLUS »	Prendre un bain dans la brousse, sous les étoiles

A sense of place...
Makalali Private Game Reserve, Limpopo Province

A sense of place

It is said that the best architecture is that which reflects a real sense of place.

The red clay structures at Makalali are a potent mix of modern and ethnic style. Their thatched roofs rise up through towering jackalberry trees, roofs that have been crowned with straw to look like a traditional village. Inside the luxury bush camp is where the resemblance ends. Natural textures blend with African craftsmanship, to create a look that is at once both rustic and opulent. The surrounds may be cultured, but just beyond the camp there is plenty of wild and beastly behaviour going on.

The camp lies on shady riverbanks, in a private game reserve within thousands of acres of open savannah grassland. Lion, leopard, cheetah, elephant, giraffe, white rhino, zebra, antelope and an array of small mammals make their home in these grasslands.

This is the new safari age, one where the aim is to protect the environment and the stunning local animal life. Here, visitors can experience a sense of close connection with nature, yet live at a safe distance from it, guarded from curious wildlife coming too near.

Book to pack: "The White Lioness: A Mystery" by Henning Mankell

Makalali Private Game Reserve
P.O. Box 809
Hoedspruit 1380
Limpopo Province
South Africa
Tel: + 27 (15) 793 93 00
Fax: + 27 (15) 793 17 39
E-mail: reservations@aha.travel
Website: www.makalali.co.za
www.great-escapes-hotels.com

DIRECTIONS	Daily flights from Johannesburg to Hoedspruit and Phalaborwa. By road about a 4.5-hour drive from Johannesburg, or arrive in a small aircraft at the private airstrip
RATES	$$$
ROOMS	Four separate 12-bed camps
FOOD	Award-winning cuisine
HISTORY	Opened in July 1996
X-FACTOR	Stunning architecture and animal life

Ein Ort mit Seele

Man sagt, dass die beste Architektur diejenige ist, welche den wahren Geist eines Ortes widerspiegelt.

Die roten Lehmelemente in Makalali stellen eine ausdrucksstarke Verbindung zwischen modernem und ethnischem Stil dar. Strohgedeckte Dächer ragen durch gewaltige »Schakalbeerenbäume« empor, ihre Spitzen wurden mit Stroh verziert, damit sie wie ein traditionelles Dorf wirken. Betritt man das luxuriöse Buschcamp, wird man jedoch schnell feststellen, dass das so ziemlich die einzige Ähnlichkeit ist. Die Verbindung natürlicher Stoffe mit afrikanischen Kunsthandwerke erzeugt eine rustikale, aber zugleich opulente Atmosphäre. Die unmittelbare Umgebung ist kultiviert, doch direkt hinter den Grenzen des Camps spielt sich das raue und wilde Leben der Tierwelt ab. Das Camp liegt auf schattigen Flussbänken in einem privaten Wildpark und ist umgeben von Tausenden von Morgen weiter Graslandschaft. In dieser Savanne sind Löwen, Leoparden, Geparden, Elefanten, Giraffen, weiße Nashörner, Zebras, Antilopen und eine Reihe kleiner Säugetiere zu Hause.

Eine neue Ära des Safaritourismus ist angebrochen, eine Ära, die sich den Schutz der Natur und den Erhalt der beeindruckenden Tierwelt, die dort lebt, zum Ziel gesetzt hat. Besucher können hier ein Gefühl der engen Verbundenheit mit der Natur erfahren und dabei doch in sicherer Entfernung bleiben, sodass ihnen neugierige Tiere trotzdem nicht allzu nah kommen.

Buchtipp: »Die weiße Löwin« von Henning Mankell

Le bon goût sauvage

On dit d'une architecture réussie qu'elle reflète le véritable esprit d'un lieu.

Les structures en argile rouge de Makalali sont un puissant mélange de modernité et d'ethnicité. Leurs toits de chaume, qui pointent çà et là au travers d'imposants arbres jackalberry, sont couronnés de paille pour évoquer un village traditionnel. Cependant, la ressemblance se limite à l'aspect extérieur. C'est en effet dans un camp de brousse luxueux que vous entrerez, où les textures naturelles associées à l'art africain créent une ambiance à la fois rustique et opulente. Les environs du camp sont cultivés, mais un peu plus loin le territoire appartient aux animaux sauvages et la loi de la jungle prévaut.

Le camp est situé sur les berges ombragées d'une rivière, dans une réserve naturelle privée qui s'étend sur des milliers d'hectares de savane où vivent des lions, des léopards, des guépards, des éléphants, des girafes, des rhinocéros blancs, des zèbres, des antilopes et toutes sortes de petits mammifères.

Nous sommes entrés dans une ère où safari rime avec protection de l'environnement et de l'extraordinaire faune locale. Ici, les visiteurs se sentiront très proches de la nature tout en restant à une distance respecteuse garantissant leur sécurité face à des animaux qui, curieux, pourraient s'approcher trop près.

Livre à emporter : « Silences africains » de Peter Matthiessen

ANREISE	Tägliche Flüge von Johannesburg nach Hoedspruit und Phalaborwa. Mit dem Wagen etwa viereinhalbstündige Fahrt von Johannesburg aus. Anreise im kleinen Flugzeug zum privaten Flugplatz möglich
PREIS	$$$
ZIMMER	Vier separate 12-Betten Camps
KÜCHE	Preisgekrönt!
GESCHICHTE	Eröffnet im Juli 1996
X-FAKTOR	Betörende Architektur und Tierwelt

ACCÈS	Vols quotidiens en partance de Johannesburg jusqu'à Hoedspruit et Phalaborwa. À 4H30 en voiture de Johannesburg. Possibilité d'emprunter une avionnette jusqu'à la piste d'atterrissage privée
PRIX	$$$
CHAMBRES	Quatre camps séparés comptant chacun 12 lits
RESTAURATION	Cuisine récompensée par plusieurs prix
HISTOIRE	Ouvert en juillet 1996
LES « PLUS »	Architecture et faune exceptionnelles

Cape majestic...

Plettenberg Park, Plettenberg Bay

Plettenberg Park,
Plettenberg Bay

Cape majestic

Both fish and fowl frequent here – on one side spouting whales, on the other wild ducks.

Plettenberg Bay is on the southern cape of South Africa, in the heart of the Garden Route, which covers several hundred miles of coastline. As so much of the coast is elevated, it is ideal for whale watching. One of the best places to spot the marine mammoths is gazing out to sea from Plettenberg Park Hotel. Situated within the most exclusive private nature reserve on the Cape, the hotel is set high up on the majestic cliffs of this dramatically beautiful coastline. Impressive views of the pounding Indian Ocean below are counterbalanced by the calm lakeshore scene of an inland wild duck sanctuary, and the stylish, restful interior. This is an all-weather hotel, basking in sunshine during the summer, but equally fine in winter, with blazing log fires keeping guests snug in luxury at the centre of the wild and spectacular surrounds. Bird watching – the park is part of the black eagle's hunting ground – game trails, snorkelling and fishing are a few of the many pastimes on offer.

Just staying put on the terrace and scanning the sea for whales would be time well spent.

Book to pack: "Long Walk to Freedom" by Nelson Mandela

Plettenberg Park	
P.O. Box 167	
Plettenberg Bay 6600	
South Africa	
Tel: + 27 (44) 533 90 67	
Fax: + 27 (44) 533 90 92	
E-mail: info@plettenbergpark.co.za	
Website: www.plettenbergpark.co.za	
www.great-escapes-hotels.com	

DIRECTIONS	Daily flights from Cape Town and Johannesburg to Port Elizabeth and George Airports. Smaller charter aircraft can land at Plettenberg Park airport
RATES	$$
ROOMS	9 double rooms
FOOD	The hotel's speciality is seafood – not whale though!
HISTORY	Originally built as a private holiday home and converted into a hotel in 1996
X-FACTOR	Whale sightings

Majestätische Klippen

Hier gibt es sowohl Fische, als auch Federvieh – wasser-
schnaubende Wale auf der einen Seite, wilde Enten auf der
anderen.

Plettenberg Bay liegt am südlichen Kap Afrikas inmitten
der Garden Route, die sich über mehrere hundert Kilometer
entlang der Küste erstreckt. Da ein großer Teil der Küsten-
linie erhöht ist, eignet sie sich hervorragend zur Walbe-
obachtung. Einer der am geeignetsten Plätze, um die
Meeressäuger zu erspähen, ist das Hotel Plettenberg Park
das innerhalb des exklusivsten privaten Naturschutzgebiets
am Kap liegt. Es erhebt sich hoch droben auf den majestäti-
schen Klippen dieser dramatisch schönen Küste.

Zu dem beeindruckenden Ausblick auf den rauen Indischen
Ozean, der unterhalb der Klippen wogt, bilden das ruhige
Seeufer des Wildentenschutzgebietes im Landesinneren
sowie die stilvoll gemütliche Einrichtung einen harmoni-
schen Ausgleich. Es ist ein Hotel für jedes Wetter, sonnig
warm im Sommer, doch ebenso reizvoll im Winter, wenn
glühende Holzscheite die Gäste inmitten dieser wilden und
eindrucksvollen Umgebung in behaglichen Luxus hüllen.

Das Beobachten von Vögeln – der Park ist Jagdgrund des
Schwarzadlers – das Erforschen der Wildpfade, das Schnor-
cheln und Fischen sind nur einige der vielen Möglichkeiten,
um sich die Zeit zu vertreiben.

Selbst wer einfach nur auf der Terrasse liegt und dabei seine
Augen auf der Suche nach Walen über das Meer schweifen
lässt, hat seine Zeit gut genutzt.

Buchtipp: »Der lange Weg zur Freiheit « von Nelson Mandela

Le Cap, majestueux

Les poissons et les oiseaux sont nombreux dans cette région.
On peut admirer d'un côté des baleines et leurs jets d'eau et,
de l'autre, des canards sauvages.

La baie de Plettenberg est située à la pointe méridionale
de l'Afrique du Sud, au cœur de la Route des Jardins, qui
s'étend sur plusieurs centaines de kilomètres de littoral.
Une grande partie de la côte étant surélevée, le site est idéal
pour l'observation des baleines. L'un des meilleurs endroits
pour scruter la mer et apercevoir ces mammouths marins
est l'Hôtel Plettenberg Park. Situé dans la réserve naturelle
privée la plus luxueuse du Cap, il se dresse au sommet
des falaises majestueuses de ce magnifique littoral. La vue
impressionnante sur l'Océan Indien qui martèle la côte en
contrebas est pondérée par le spectacle paisible des rives
d'un lac où les canards sauvages ont trouvé refuge et par
l'intérieur élégant et confortable de l'hôtel, entièrement
décoré de cuir. Baigné de soleil tout l'été, celui-ci est tout
aussi agréable l'hiver grâce à ses grands feux de cheminée
qui permettent aux résidents de rester bien au chaud au
centre d'un cadre tout à la fois luxueux, sauvage et spectaculaire. L'observation des oiseaux (le parc est l'un des terrains
de chasse de l'aigle noir), les randonnées d'observation de
la faune, la plongée avec tuba et la pêche ne sont que
quelques-unes des nombreuses activités proposées.

Si vous préférez rester sur la terrasse et sonder l'horizon
à la recherche de baleines, vous ne perdrez pas non plus
votre temps.

**Livre à emporter : « Un long chemin vers la liberté » de Nelson
Mandela**

ANREISE	Täglich Flüge von Kapstadt und Johannesburg nach Port Elizabeth und George Flughafen. Kleinere Chartermaschinen können auf dem Plettenberg Park Flugplatz landen	ACCÈS	Vols quotidiens du Cap et de Johannesburg aux aéroports de Port Elizabeth et George. Avions charters plus petits pour l'aéroport de la baie de Plettenberg
PREIS	$$	PRIX	$$
ZIMMER	9 Doppelzimmer	CHAMBRES	9 chambres doubles
KÜCHE	Spezialität des Hotels sind Fisch und Meeresfrüchte – kein Wal!	RESTAURATION	Les fruits de mer sont la spécialité de l'hôtel. La baleine n'est pas au menu !
GESCHICHTE	Ursprünglich ein privates Feriendomizil, zum Hotel umgebaut im Jahre 1996	HISTOIRE	Construit à l'origine pour servir de maison de vacances privée, le bâtiment est devenu un hôtel en 1996
X-FAKTOR	Walbeobachtung	LES « PLUS »	L'observation des baleines

Cheap and chic...
Bloomestate, Swellendam

Bloomestate, Swellendam

Cheap and chic

A place where there are four seasons on one day? No, that is not the climate here; it's simply that each of the four guest suites has a seasonal theme. You could stay for a whole year and experience each one.

Whatever the weather is like where you are now, this chic guesthouse presents you with the opposite of it. You can choose the season inside. Winter is a good deal more appealing here than in most places.

The outside ambience is not as easy to select, but the climate is more often than not mild, whatever the time of year. Bloomestate is on the way to, and from, the Garden Route; a hideaway hotel set in a lush garden of its own. You can unwind here in this calming modern ambience. A spell lounging by the poolside just reading a book could be all you need to do. But if you do want to go out, Bloomestate borders one of the Cape's most attractive old towns. Swellendam is the third-oldest settlement in the country; its Cape Dutch and Victorian style buildings are a sign of its rich history. National parks and wineries are nearby; and this is the home of the graceful blue crane, the country's national bird.

It has been said that in nature, light creates colour, while artists use colour to create light. The landscape of rolling fields and stately mountains changes colour along with the seasons, and each interior here is creatively painted to reflect them.

Book to pack: "Cry, the Beloved Country: A Story of Comfort in Desolation" by Alan Paton

Bloomestate	
276 Voortrekstreet	
P.O. Box 672	
Swellendam 6740	
South Africa	
Tel: + 27 (28) 514 29 84	
Fax: + 27 (28) 514 38 22	
E-mail: info@ bloomestate.com	
Website: www.bloomestate.com	
www.great-escapes-hotels.com	

DIRECTIONS	200km/124 m from both Cape Town and George, from the N2 highway take the R60, at 4-stop turn right
RATES	$
ROOMS	4 suites
FOOD	Breakfast only: fresh fruit salad with fruits of the seasons, yoghurt, choice of cereals, freshly baked croissants and whole wheat bread, toast, homemade jams, eggs
HISTORY	First blossomed in 2002
X-FACTOR	Contemporary African chic

Cheap and chic

Wie? Ein Ort, an dem man an einem einzigen Tag vier Jahreszeiten erleben kann? Keine Angst, dies ist keine Beschreibung der klimatischen Bedingungen dieses Landes, sondern der Suiten: Jede von ihnen ist thematisch nach einer bestimmten Jahreszeit gestaltet worden. So können Sie problemlos ein ganzes Jahr hier verbringen und jede von ihnen kennen lernen.

Wie auch immer das Wetter an ihrem Aufenthaltsort, sein mag, diese elegante Pension kann Ihnen das genaue Gegenteil davon bieten. Sie selbst wählen die Jahreszeit aus. Der Winter ist hier übrigens sehr viel angenehmer als in den meisten anderen Ländern.

Das Außenklima lässt sich selbstverständlich nicht ganz so leicht bestimmen, doch unabhängig von der Jahreszeit ist es hier meist sehr mild. Bloomestate liegt an der »Garden Route«, ein kleines verstecktes Hotel inmitten eines sattgrünen Gartens. In diesem ruhigen, modernen Ambiente können Sie sich entspannen, indem Sie beispielsweise ganz einfach ein Weilchen am Pool liegen und in einem Buch schmökern. Ebenso können Sie aber auch etwas unternehmen, denn Bloomestate liegt am Rande einer der ältesten und schönsten Städte des Kaps. Swellendam ist die drittälteste Siedlung des Landes. Dass sie auf eine lange Geschichte zurückblicken kann, lässt sich an den Gebäuden im kapholländischen und viktorianischen Stil ablesen. Ganz in der Nähe befinden sich Nationalparks und Weinberge. Hier lebt auch der Landesvogel Südafrikas, der blaue Kranich.

In der Natur, sagt man, bringt Licht Farbe hervor, wohingegen Künstler Farbe benutzen, um Lichteffekte zu erzeugen. Die hiesige Landschaft mit ihren hügeligen Feldern und eindrucksvollen Bergen ändert mit den Jahreszeiten die Farbe. Die Innengestaltung der Suiten soll dies widerspiegeln.

Buchtipp: »Denn sie sollen getröstet werden« von Alan Paton

Chic et pas cher

Si vous pensez voir ici défiler les quatre saisons en une seule journée, vous vous trompez. En revanche, chacune des quatre suites du Bloomestate a pour thème une saison particulière. Vous pourriez séjourner à l'hôtel toute l'année et changer de chambre et de saison au gré de vos envies. Quel que soit le temps actuellement dans votre lieu de résidence, cette élégante pension de famille vous propose d'en changer. Vous constaterez aussi que l'hiver est ici plus agréable qu'ailleurs.

Impossible par contre de choisir le climat extérieur, ce qui n'est pas vraiment un problème puisque celui-ci est tempéré pendant pratiquement toute l'année. Bloomestate, qui se trouve sur le chemin de la Route des Jardins, est un hôtel retiré installé au cœur d'un jardin luxuriant. Son atmosphère paisible et son cadre moderne invitent à la détente. Un moment à paresser au bord de la piscine, un livre à la main, est peut-être juste ce qu'il vous faut. Mais si vous souhaitez sortir, Bloomestate jouxte l'une des vieilles villes les plus intéressantes du Cap. Troisième ville du pays en termes d'ancienneté, Swellendam présente en effet des bâtiments de style victorien et hollandais qui témoignent de sa riche histoire. Les parcs nationaux et les entreprises vinicoles ne sont qu'à un jet de pierre, et la région abrite l'oiseau national, l'élégante grue de paradis.

On dit que dans la nature, c'est la lumière qui crée la couleur et que les artistes utilisent la couleur pour rendre la lumière. Ici, le paysage formé par les terres aux formes gracieuses et les montagnes majestueuses se teinte de nouvelles nuances au fil des saisons, des nuances que reflètent avec originalité les couleurs utilisées à l'intérieur de chaque suite.

Livre à emporter : « Pleure, ô pays bien-aimé » d'Alan Paton

ANREISE	200 km von Kapstadt und George entfernt. Vom N2 Highway auf die R60, an der vierten Kreuzung rechts abbiegen
PREIS	$
ZIMMER	4 Suiten
KÜCHE	Nur Frühstück: frische Obstsalate mit Früchten der Saison, Joghurt, einer Auswahl an Müslis, frisch gebakkenen Croissants und Vollkornweizenbrot, Toast, hausgemachten Marmeladen, Eiern
GESCHICHTE	Erblüht im Jahr 2002
X-FAKTOR	Zeitgemäßer afrikanischer Chic

ACCÈS	À 200 km du Cap et de George. Prendre la N2, puis la R60 et tourner à droite au quatrième stop
PRIX	$
CHAMBRES	4 suites
RESTAURATION	Petit déjeuner uniquement : salade de fruits frais de la saison, yaourt, choix de céréales, pain complet et croissants tout juste sortis du four, pain grillé, confitures maison, œufs
HISTOIRE	Ouvert en 2002
LES « PLUS »	Style contemporain et chic typiquement africain

Town and country...
Kensington Place, Cape Town

Town and country

Only two of Henry VIII's six wives lost their heads in the real sense. The other four were able to avoid such a blunt end to their unions. All of them are recalled here, for the rooms at Kensington Place are each named after one of the monarch's wives or his daughters. And it seems a fitting response to their varied characters that each room should have a distinct style. There are, of course, some common themes. One is the choice of materials. Suede, silk and leather are featured, just some of the rich fabrics long favoured by royalty – and those who are at home with luxury. And plush colours like whisky, chocolate and cinnamon mixed with cream please the eye as much as those flavours please the taste. The design is a blend of Africa and Europe, a fusion of textures and fabrics to great effect.

A lush garden surrounds the hotel, which is in a quiet residential area of Capetown, deemed to be one of the most prestigious in the city. The views from here are duly majestic too. Although its setting is an urban one, the outlook from the terrace is more of a stately vista than might be expected; scenes of the harbour and the mountains meet the eye. If guests wish to venture forth to the world outside the gates, beaches, gardens and wineries are within reach. And although not visible from here, quite close by a great animal kingdom lies in wait.

Book to pack: "July's People" by Nadine Gordimer

Kensington Place

38 Kensington Crescent
Higgovale
Cape Town 8001
South Africa
Tel: + 27 (21) 424 47 44
Fax: + 27 (21) 424 18 10
E-mail: info@kensingtonplace.co.za
Website: www.kensingtonplace.co.za
www.great-escapes-hotels.com

DIRECTIONS	Approximately 24 km/15 m from Cape Town International Airport
RATES	$
ROOMS	8 double rooms with private terraces
FOOD	A menu fit for monarchs and other crowned heads
HISTORY	Opened in 1997, far too late for Henry VIII to visit in person
X-FACTOR	A perfect match between town and country

Stadt und Land

Nur zwei der sechs Frauen von Henry VIII. verloren ihren
Kopf im wörtlichen Sinne. Den anderen vier Gemahlinnen
gelang es, ein solch stumpfes Ende ihrer ehelichen Verbindung zu umgehen. Die Räume des Kensington Place sind
benannt nach den Frauen des Monarchen beziehungsweise
nach seinen Töchtern und es scheint eine angemessene Ant-
wort auf deren unterschiedliche Charaktere zu sein, dass jeder
der Räume in einem anderen Stil eingerichtet ist. Dennoch
gibt es einige Gemeinsamkeiten, zum Beispiel in der Verwen-
dung von Wildleder, Seide und Leder, solch prächtige Stoffe
wurden schon immer von Königen und solchen, die im Luxus
leben, favorisiert. Und die edlen mit Cremetönen versetzten
Whisky-, Schokoladen- und Zimtfarbenen gefallen dem Auge
ebenso wie sie betörende Düfte hervorrufen. Die Inneneinan-
richtung mischt afrikanische und europäische Elemente, eine
äußerst effektvolle Verbindung von Stoffen und Geweben.
Ein üppiger Garten umgibt das Hotel, das sich in einer ruhigen Wohngegend, einer der privilegiertesten von Kapstadt,
befindet. Dementsprechend majestätisch ist auch der Ausblick, den man von hier aus genießen kann. Obwohl das
Hotel in der Stadt liegt, ist der Blick von der Terrasse beein-
druckender, als man zunächst glauben möchte, wenn man
das Auge weit über Hafenbuchten und Bergketten hinweg-
schweifen lässt. Gäste, welche die Welt außerhalb der Tore
kennen lernen möchten, können dies tun: Strände, Gärten
und Weinberge liegen ebenso wie eine großartige Tierwelt,
ganz in der Nähe.

Buchtipp: »July's Leute« von Nadine Gordimer

La ville verdure

Seules deux des six épouses d'Henry VIII perdirent la tête,
au sens propre. Les quatre autres surent échapper à cette
façon quelque peu abrupte de mettre fin à leur union.
Kensington Place a souhaité toutes les évoquer en donnant
le nom des femmes ou des filles du roi aux chambres de
l'hôtel. À l'image de ces dames, chaque chambre a un caractère bien particulier. Certains éléments sont bien sûr com-
muns à toutes : les matières somptueuses par exemple, avec
le daim, la soie et le cuir, pour lesquelles les familles royales
et ceux qui aiment le luxe ont toujours eu une préférence ;
les superbes couleurs, avec de riches tons whisky, chocolat
et cannelle qui, associés à la couleur crème, flattent le regard
tout autant que les parfums qu'ils évoquent ravissent le
palais. Le décor est un mélange d'Afrique et d'Europe, une
fusion de textures et d'étoffes du plus bel effet.
L'hôtel, situé dans une zone résidentielle tranquille du Cap,
l'une des plus prestigieuses de la ville, se trouve au centre
d'un jardin luxuriant. Le spectacle qui s'offre aux yeux des
résidents de l'hôtel est majestueux : le cadre est urbain,
mais la vue depuis la terrasse, sur le port et les montagnes
proches, est plus impressionnante qu'on pourrait le croire.
Vous souhaitez vous aventurer à l'extérieur de l'enceinte ?
Les plages, les jardins et les établissements vinicoles ne sont
qu'à un jet de pierre.
Vous pouvez par ailleurs admirer une faune extraordinaire
et variée, invisible depuis l'hôtel mais pourtant toute proche.

Livre à emporter : « Ceux de July » de Nadine Gordimer

ANREISE	Etwa 24 km vom Cape Town International Airport
PREIS	$
ZIMMER	8 Doppelzimmer mit eigener Terrasse
KÜCHE	Eine Speisekarte für Könige und andere gekrönte Häupter
GESCHICHTE	Eröffnet im Jahr 1997 und somit viel zu spät, um von Henry VIII. persönlich besucht worden zu sein
X-FAKTOR	Eine perfektes Zusammenspiel von Stadt und Land

ACCÈS	À environ 24 Km de l'aéroport international du Cap
PRIX	$
CHAMBRES	8 chambres doubles avec terrasse privée
RESTAURATION	Menu digne des monarques et autres têtes couronnées
HISTOIRE	Ouvert en 1997, bien trop tard pour qu'Henry VIII puisse le visiter
LES « PLUS »	Alliance parfaite entre ville et campagne

Soul searching...
Sossusvlei Wilderness Camp, Namib Naukluft Park

Soul searching

"God created countries with water to enable mankind to live there, and deserts so that they may find their souls." A Namibian proverb.

Namibia has been called "the land that God made in anger." In a country made up of sweltering desert and mountains of sand and rock, man seems out of place. Yet the great sum of sand, the space and the vast silence draws us here.

The Namib Desert is the oldest in the world; at its heart are the Sossusvlei, some of the highest dunes on earth. Rich in contrast of colour and shape, the deep crescents are one of the most stunning sights in Africa. Great waves of them spread out in every direction, as far as the eye can see. When the sun sets, the massive dunes change from pale apricot to bright orange to deep red. Above, against a clear dark sky, the Milky Way sweeps across in a dazzling light show.

At the entrance to this vast backdrop, is the Sossusvlei Wilderness Camp. Set close to the top of a hill, the little camp merges into the environment, built as it is of rock, timber and thatch. Its bungalows are a cool respite from the heat of the desert. Each has a commanding view out towards the plains and mountains. In the distance are the dunes.

The sheer physical beauty of the desert landscape is the main lure; seeing game much less so. But there are animals to be seen, more often ones that blend into the background, like the cape fox, the aardvark, springbok, and oryx. Eagles fly high above the ostrich – with its head in the sand and out.

Books to pack: "Wind, Sand and Stars" by Antoine de Saint Exupéry

"Desert and Wilderness" by Henryk Sienkiewicz

Sossusvlei Wilderness Camp
Namib Naukluft Park
Namibia
Tel: + 27 (11) 888 40 37
Fax: + 27 (11) 888 10 41
E-mail: enquiries@adventure.co.za
Website: www.africanadrenalin.co.za
www.great-escapes-hotels.com

DIRECTIONS	20 kms/12.5 miles south-east from Sesriem, and a one-hour flight from Windhoek International Airport
RATES	$$
ROOMS	8 double rooms, 1 honeymoon chalet
HISTORY	Opened in 1998
FOOD	Appetising and sand-free fare
X-FACTOR	Taking a balloon ride over the stunning canyon and dunes of this ancient desert

Seelensuche

»Gott hat Länder voll Wasser geschaffen, damit die Menschen dort leben können und Wüsten, damit sie dort ihre Seele erkennen...« Altes namibianisches Sprichwort.

Namibia nennt man »das Land, das Gott im Zorn erschuf«. Menschliches Leben scheint in einem Land, das aus flimmernd heißen Wüsten und Sand- und Felsgebirgen besteht, fehl am Platz zu sein. Dennoch sind es gerade die Massen von Sand, die Weiträumigkeit und die grenzenlose Stille, die uns hierher locken.

Die Namib Wüste ist die älteste der Welt, mitten in ihrem Inneren befinden sich die Sossusvlei, die zu den höchsten Dünen der Erde zählen. Mit ihren Farb- und Formkontrasten gehören diese unergründlichen Halbmonde zu den überwältigendsten Sehenswürdigkeiten Afrikas. So weit das Auge reicht, setzen sie sich wellenartig in alle Himmelsrichtungen fort. Bei Sonnenuntergang werden die gewaltigen Dünen zunächst in ein zartes apricotfarbenes, und kurz darauf in helloranges und schließlich blutrotes Licht getaucht. Und über all dies fegt die Milchstrasse wie eine glitzernde Lichtshow am dunklen, klaren Himmel hinweg.

Am Eingang zu dieser riesigen Kulisse befindet sich das Sossusvlei Wilderness Camp. Da es aus Fels, Holz und Dachstroh gebaut ist, verschmilzt das kleine, nahe dem Gipfel eines Hügels gelegene Lager mit der Umgebung. Seine Bungalows bieten eine kühle Ruhepause von der Hitze der Wüste. Von jedem Bungalow aus bietet sich ein eindrucksvoller Ausblick auf die Ebenen und Berge hinaus, und in der Ferne liegen die Dünen.

Was diesen Ort so verlockend macht, ist vor allem die bloße Schönheit der Wüstenlandschaft und weniger die Möglichkeit, auf Safari zu gehen. Dennoch gibt es durchaus Tiere zu beobachten, meist solche, die sich gegen ihren Hintergrund schwer ausmachen lassen, wie der Kamafuchs, das Erdferkel, der Springbock und die Säbelantilope. Adler fliegen über Strauße hinweg, die den Kopf im Sand stecken haben, oder auch nicht.

Buchtipps: »Wind, Sand und Sterne« von Antoine de Saint Exupéry
»Desert and Wilderness« von Henryk Sienkiewicz

Introspection

« Dieu a créé des pays pleins d'eau pour que les hommes puissent y vivre et des déserts pour qu'ils puissent y découvrir leur âme. » Proverbe namibien.

On appelle la Namibie « la terre créée par un Dieu en colère ». Dans ce pays au climat torride fait de déserts et de montagnes de sable et de roche, l'homme ne semble pas à sa place. Pourtant, ce sont précisément les étendues de sable, l'espace et le profond silence qui nous attirent dans cette région.

Au cœur du désert de Namib, le plus ancien de la planète, se trouvent les dunes de Sossusvlei, qui sont parmi les plus hautes du monde. Ces grands croissants, qui se caractérisent par la richesse du contraste des couleurs et des formes, sont l'un des spectacles les plus impressionnants d'Afrique. Les énormes vagues de sable s'étendent dans toutes les directions, à perte de vue.

Au coucher du soleil, ces dunes immenses passent de l'abricot pâle à l'orange vif, puis au rouge profond. Par nuit claire, la Voie lactée balaie le ciel en un jeu de lumières éblouissant. Sossusvlei Wilderness Camp s'élève là où commence ce vaste désert. Installé à proximité du sommet d'une colline, ce camp de taille réduite, fait de roche, de bois et de chaume, se fond dans le paysage. Après la chaleur du désert, la fraicheur des bungalows constitue un répit bienvenu. Chacun d'eux offre une vue panoramique sur les plaines et les montagnes, et sur les dunes au loin.

Le principal attrait du site est l'extraordinaire beauté du désert. En revanche, la faune y est rare. Il est toutefois possible d'apercevoir quelques animaux, surtout des espèces qui se confondent avec leur environnement, telles que le renard du Cap, l'oryctérope, le springbok ou l'oryx. Les aigles survolent les autruches, que vous verrez en mouvement ou immobiles, la tête enfouie dans le sable.

Livres à emporter : « Terre des Hommes » d'Antoine de Saint Exupéry
« Le désert et la gloire » de Fathallah Sâyigh

ANREISE	20 km südöstlich von Sesriem, und einstündiger Flug von Windhuk International Airport	ACCÈS	À 20 Km au sud-est de Sesriem et à une heure en avion de Windhoek International Airport
PREIS	$$	PRIX	$$
ZIMMER	8 Doppelzimmer, 1 Hochzeitszimmer	CHAMBRES	8 chambres doubles et un chalet lune de miel
GESCHICHTE	Eröffnet im Jahr 1998	RESTAURATION	Appétissante et garantie sans sable !
KÜCHE	Appetitliche und sandlose Speisen	HISTOIRE	Ouvert en 1998
X-FAKTOR	Eine Ballonfahrt über den beeindruckenden Canyon und die Dünen dieser alten Wüste	LES « PLUS »	Excursion en ballon au-dessus du superbe canyon et des magnifiques dunes de ce désert ancestral

The beat goes on...
Ankobra Beach, Axim

Ankobra Beach, Axim

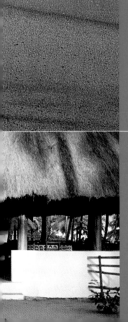

The beat goes on

Most people are not keen on neighbours who play the drums. The sound travels; a learner can drive listeners 'round the bend'.

At Ankobra Beach Resort drumming is encouraged; in fact, they teach it to the guests here. Free lessons in drumming, and in dancing, are to hand. It is in the age-old African kind. It was from this continent that percussion came; Africa is the source of the beat. But this is also a quiet place; there are no amplifiers. Lessons are short and during the day. The sound of the sea, and the sigh of the coconut palms stroked by the breeze, muffle most noise.

The group of round bungalows is much like an African village. Clustered amongst coconut trees, on the edge of a sandy beach, at first glance they appear to be quite small. Looks can be deceptive. As if by magic, they are larger inside than they seem from outside. As the river meets the ocean here, Ankobra Beach has a broad motto; "where Africa meets the world." This guides the resort owners and the staff. They want time spent here to give an insight to African culture and current life; a life led outside the cities. The focus is on the beauty and grace that Africa still offers. Beauty also abounds in the nature here.

Some of the history is not so lovely. Many people left Ghana from this Atlantic coast, forced aboard slave ships; but they took their rhythms with them.

Books to pack: "Search Sweet Country" by B. Kojo Laing
"The Beautiful Ones Are Not Yet Born" by Ayi Kwei Armah

Ankobra Beach
P.O. Box 79
Axim
Ghana
Tel: + 233 (31) 923 21
Email: ankobra_beach@hotmail.com
Website: www.ankobrabeach.de
www.great-escapes-hotels.com

DIRECTIONS	A 4-hour drive west from Accra Airport
RATES	$
ROOMS	10 rooms, 6 bungalows
FOOD	African and international cooking
HISTORY	Opened in 1996
X-FACTOR	The slower, simpler, and gentle pace of life

Im Rhythmus der Wellen

Auf Trommelspielende Nachbarn sind die Wenigsten erpicht. Den Klang von Trommeln hört man durch Wände, und schon so mancher Trommelschüler mag seine unfreiwilligen Zuhörer in den Wahnsinn getrieben haben.

Im Ankobra Beach Resort hingegen ist Trommeln erwünscht, um genauer zu sein, lehrt man hier die Gäste das Trommelspielen. Es besteht die Möglichkeit, an kostenlosen Trommel- und Tanzstunden nach altafrikanischer Tradition teilzunehmen. Auf diesem Kontinent ist die Perkussion zu Hause, Afrika ist sozusagen die Mutter des Rhythmus. Gleichzeitig ist dies jedoch auch ein ruhiger Ort und es gibt keine Verstärker. Die Übungsstunden dauern nur kurz und werden tagsüber abgehalten. Das Geräusch des Meeres und das Rascheln der Kokosnusspalmen im Wind verschlucken den Großteil der Klänge.

Die Gruppe runder Bungalows erinnert stark an ein afrikanisches Dorf. Geduckt zwischen Kokosnussbäumen und am Rande eines Sandstrandes, wirken sie auf den ersten Blick relativ klein. Umso erstaunter ist man, wenn man beim Betreten ihre stattliche Größe erfährt. Da der Fluss hier ins Meer mündet gibt es in Ankobra Beach ein Motto: »Wo Afrika und die Welt zusammentreffen«. Das ist der Leitspruch für die Besitzer der Anlage und das Personal. Sie wollen, dass die Zeit, die man hier verbringt, einen Einblick in die afrikanische Kultur und das jetzige Leben vermittelt; ein Leben außerhalb der Städte. Im Mittelpunkt stehen die Schönheit und Anmut, die Afrika immer noch bietet. Schönheit findet man hier in der natürlichen Umgebung überall.

Aber dieser Teil Afrikas hat im Lauf der Geschichte auch weniger schöne Zeiten erlebt. Auf Sklavenschiffe verfrachtet mussten viele Menschen Ghana von dieser Küste aus verlassen, doch ihre Rhythmen nahmen sie mit.

Buchtipps: »Die Sonnensucher« von B. Kojo Laing
»Die Schönen sind noch nicht geboren« von Ayi Kwei Armah

Au rythme des vagues

La plupart d'entre nous n'apprécieraient pas d'avoir pour voisin un joueur de tambour. Le son se propage, et un joueur débutant peut rendre complètement fous des auditeurs non consentants.

À Ankobra Beach Resort, la pratique de cet instrument est encouragée. De fait, des cours de percussion et de danse gratuits sont proposés. Bien sûr, ces cours portent sur les percussions africaines traditionnelles. C'est sur ce continent en effet que sont nés ces instruments. C'est en Afrique que se trouve l'origine du rythme. Mais ne vous inquiétez pas. L'endroit peut aussi être silencieux. Il n'y a pas d'amplificateurs, et les leçons sont courtes et ont lieu pendant la journée. Pour le reste, le bruit de la mer et le murmure des cocotiers caressés par la brise couvrent la plupart des bruits.

L'ensemble formé par les bungalows circulaires ressemble beaucoup à un village africain. Regroupés à l'ombre des cocotiers, au bord de la plage, ceux-ci paraissent de taille relativement réduite à première vue. Mais les apparences sont parfois trompeuses. Il suffit d'y entrer et, comme par enchantement, on découvre un intérieur plus spacieux que ce à quoi l'on pouvait s'attendre. Ankobra Beach se trouve à la jonction d'un fleuve et de l'océan. De là peut-être sa devise, « là où l'Afrique rencontre le monde », qui guide à tout moment les propriétaires de l'hôtel et le personnel.

Pour eux, un séjour à Ankobra Beach doit être l'occasion de découvrir la culture et le mode de vie actuel en Afrique, loin de la ville. L'accent est mis sur la beauté et la grâce qui sont, encore de nos jours, caractéristiques de l'Afrique. Et cette beauté est partout présente dans le paysage environnant.

L'Histoire, elle, est moins reluisante. Cette côte de l'Atlantique a vu de nombreuses personnes quitter le Ghana à bord de négriers. Les percussions faisaient elles aussi partie du voyage.

Livre à emporter : « L'âge d'or n'est pas pour demain » d'Ayi Kwei Armah

ANREISE	4-stündige Fahrt westlich von Accra Airport
PREIS	$
ZIMMER	10 Zimmer, 6 Bungalows
KÜCHE	Afrikanische und internationale Gerichte
GESCHICHTE	Eröffnet im Jahre 1996
X-FAKTOR	Die einfache und geruhsame Art zu leben

ACCÈS	À 4 heures en voiture de l'aéroport d'Accra, à l'ouest
PRIX	$
CHAMBRES	10 chambres, 6 bungalows
RESTAURATION	Cuisine africaine et internationale
HISTOIRE	Ouvert en 1996
LES « PLUS »	Un rythme de vie simple et tranquille

A dome of one's own...
Hotel Le Kambary, Bandiagara

A dome of one's own

These white domes pop up in the desert like huge beehives.
At first sight, they might look quite familiar. They will
remind science fiction fans of a "Star Wars" space colony.
But in fact it is a creative hotel on this planet, in the heart of
one of Africa's largest but least known countries, Mali. Five
hundred years ago one of the world's wealthiest nations,
now it is among the poorest. Yet it is still rich in history and
culture. In the 14th century, the Malian empire was one of
the greatest on earth, endowed with two sources of great
wealth – salt and gold. Both were equally valued, ounce for
ounce. This is the homeland of Timbuktu, a legendary city
once called 'the most distant place on earth'. It was the intel-
lectual centre of the Arab world, and a thriving commercial
city. Then it was the 'most glorious city' in medieval Africa.
Little remains of its past glory now.

Mali is famous too for its mud architecture, from great temples to whole villages, and an intriguing people, the Dogon.
Hotel Le Kambary is close to Dogon country. Aeons ago,
to ward off conversion to Islam, they fled to the cliffs of
Bandiagara, now dotted with ancient cliff dwellings and
burial sites. The worship of their ancestors, as well as their
architecture, farming ability and knowledge of the stars have
long made them a magnet for visitors.

**Books to pack: "The Fortunes of Wangrin" by Amadou
Hampate Ba
"God's Bits of Wood" by Ousmane Sembene**

Hotel Le Kambary	
Bandiagara	
Province de Mopti	
Mali	
Tel: + 223 420 388	
Fax: + 223 420 388	
E-mail: chevalblancmali@yahoo.fr	
Website: www.kambary.com	
www.great-escapes-hotels.com	

DIRECTIONS	A few minutes from Bandiagara, and aprox. 70 km/43 m from Mopti, Mali's Venice
RATES	$
ROOMS	14 rooms, 1 apartment
FOOD	The hotel restaurant Cheval-Blanc has African and European dishes on the menu
HISTORY	Designed by Italian architect Fabrizio Carola and opened in 1997. The architect's aim was to build without using wood, a scarce and expensive resource. Stone domes and arches are therefore among the main construction components
X-FACTOR	The hotel dining pods, the World Heritage site of the Dogon and the nearby Center for Traditional Medicine

Jedem seine Kuppel

Wie riesenhafte Bienenstöcke ragen diese weißen Kuppeln aus dem Wüstenboden. Auf den ersten Blick mögen sie ziemlich vertraut aussehen, zumindest für Science Fiction Fans, die sich unmittelbar an eine »Star Wars Weltraumsiedlung« erinnert fühlen.

In Wirklichkeit handelt es sich dabei um ein künstlerisches Hotel auf diesem unserem Planeten, im Herzen eines der größten und gleichzeitig unbekanntesten Länder Afrikas, Mali. War dieses Land vor rund fünfhundert Jahren eine der wohlhabendsten Nationen der Welt, so gehört es heute zu den ärmsten. Dennoch ist es immer noch reich an Geschichte und Kultur. Im 14. Jahrhundert war Mali eines der größten Imperien der Erde, gesegnet mit zwei Quellen großen Reichtums: Salz und Gold. Beides war von gleich hohem Wert, Unze für Unze. Auch liegt hier Timbuktu, die legendäre Stadt, die einst als der »abgelegenste Ort der Welt« bezeichnet wurde. Es war das intellektuelle Zentrum der arabischen Welt und eine blühende Handelsstadt. Dann wurde es bekannt, als die »prächtigste Stadt« im mittelalterlichen Afrika. Mag dieser Ruhm auch vergangen sein, so ist Mali heute noch berühmt für seine Schlammbauarchitektur, von großartigen Tempeln bis hin zu ganzen Dörfern, sowie für ein faszinierendes Volk, die Dogon. Das Hotel Le Kambary liegt nahe bei der Dogon-Region. Um einer Zwangsbekehrung zum Islam zu entgehen, flohen die Dogon vor langer Zeit in die Klippen von Bandiagara, welche nun mit uralten Klippensiedlungen und Grabstätten übersät sind. Ihre Ahnenverehrung, aber auch die für die Dogon typische Bauweise, ihr Talent beim Ackerbau und ihr Wissen über die Sterne haben die Besucher von jeher magisch angezogen.

Buchtipp: »Gottes Holzstücke« von Ousmane Sembene

Un dôme pour soi

Des dômes blancs qui émergent du désert telles des ruches géantes. Ce spectacle, qui vous sera peut-être familier, rappellera en tout cas aux fans de science-fiction une colonie spatiale de « La Guerre des Étoiles ».

Il s'agit en fait d'un hôtel original situé au cœur de l'un des pays les plus grands mais également les moins connus d'Afrique, le Mali, une nation parmi les plus riches du monde il y a cinq cent ans, et à l'heure actuelle l'une des plus pauvres. Le Mali conserve toutefois certaines richesses en matière d'histoire et de culture. Au XIVe siècle, l'empire malien était l'un des plus puissants du monde grâce à d'immenses revenus provenant du sel et de l'or, deux ressources alors considérées de valeur égale. Le Mali est aussi la patrie de Tombouctou, ville légendaire jadis qualifiée de « lieu le plus retiré du monde ». Centre intellectuel du monde arabe et cité commerciale florissante, elle était alors la « ville la plus merveilleuse » de l'Afrique médiévale. Aujourd'hui, ce glorieux passé n'est plus qu'un lointain souvenir.

Le Mali est également célèbre pour ses constructions en boue, qu'il s'agisse de grands temples ou de villages entiers, et en raison d'un peuple fascinant, les Dogons. L'hôtel Le Kambary est d'ailleurs proche du pays dogon. Il y a de cela bien des siècles, pour éviter d'être convertis à l'Islam, les Dogons s'enfuirent vers les falaises de Bandiagara où seules subsistent des habitations troglodytiques et des sépultures. Le culte des ancêtres, l'architecture ainsi que la science de l'agriculture et la connaissance des astres font de ce peuple un véritable pôle d'attraction, et ce depuis toujours.

Livre à emporter : « Les bouts de bois de Dieu » de Ousmane Sembene

ANREISE	Wenige Minuten von Bandiagara und 70 km von Mopti – dem Venedig von Mali – entfernt
PREIS	$
ZIMMER	14 Zimmer, 1 Apartment
KÜCHE	Die Karte des Hotel Restaurants Cheval-Blanc enthält sowohl afrikanische, als auch europäische Gerichte
GESCHICHTE	Entworfen von dem italienischen Architekten Fabrizio Carola; eröffnet im Jahr 1997. Ziel des Architekten war es, beim Bau auf Holz zu verzichten, da dies hier einen besonders seltenen und wertvollen Rohstoff darstellt
X-FAKTOR	Das Weltkulturerbe der Dogon und das nahegelegene Zentrum für traditionelle Medizin

ACCÈS	À quelques minutes de Bandiagara et à 70 km de Mopti, la Venise du Mali
PRIX	$
CHAMBRES	14 chambres, 1 appartement
RESTAURATION	La carte de l'hôtel restaurant Cheval-Blanc propose des mets africains et européens
HISTOIRE	Hôtel ouvert en 1997 et conçu par l'architecte italien Fabrizio Carola. Son objectif était de ne pas utiliser le bois
LES « PLUS »	Les « compartiments » du restaurant de l'hôtel, le site Dogon classé patrimoine de l'humanité et le Centre de médecine traditionnelle voisin

› **africanhistory.about.com**
Start here to learn more about this vast continent, from where we all came. A mass of subjects is covered, from archaeology, exploration, to political history and time-lines. Provides an in-depth overview and background, plus books on Africa.

› **africaadventures.com**
Tailor-made and custom-built safaris, 'showcasing the real Africa', whether it be staying in small intimate game lodges, classical tented camps, or small private ranches. Properties chosen for the warmth of the hosts, incredible wildlife and location, and the dedication of each establishment towards conservation and the local people. Special interest safaris are included.

› **ccafrica.com**
Conservation Corporation Africa is one of Africa's most comprehensive eco-tourism companies, with 30 luxurious private game lodges across South Africa, Kenya, Tanzania, Zimbabwe, Namibia and Botswana. An African safari mobile operation with a strong focus on guided and walking safaris; deeply committed in spirit and deed to the renaissance of Africa, its wildlife, and the people.

› **classicsafaris.com**
"The darkest thing about Africa has always been our ignorance of it" – American-based consultants specialising in all aspects of African safaris, including big game photo safaris, walking safaris, tiger fishing as well as deep sea fishing safaris, safaris on horseback, houseboats and balloons. Catering for different time frames, styles, and budgets.

› **cobra-verde.de**
In German, covering from north to south Africa and in-between, including Morocco, Algeria, Gambia, Mali, Ghana, Senegal, and Tunisia. A detailed tour arranger, the site is very informative on each country, with good photos and selection of places to stay.

› **eco-resorts.com**
Promoting small, unique East African – Kenya, Ruanda and Tanzania – camps and lodges, which are involved in assisting their local communities and protecting their local environment. "Be an eco-tourist and make a difference!"

› **experience-egypt.com**
Great information on Egypt's history, geography, and culture, plus transportation, touring, and links. An attractively designed site that is easy to navigate.

› **africanhistory.about.com**
Erfahren Sie hier mehr über diesen riesigen Kontinent, von dem wir alle ursprünglich abstammen. Hier wird ein breites Spektrum verschiedener Themen wie Archäologie, Entdeckungsgeschichte und politische Entwicklung mit Hilfe von Zeitleisten abgedeckt.

› **africaadventures.com**
Maßgeschneiderte und auf spezielle Bedürfnisse zugeschnittene Safaris, die das wahre Afrika zeigen wollen. Auswahlkriterien für die beschriebenen Unterkünfte sind Gastfreundschaft, außergewöhnliche Naturschönheit und Lage sowie die Entschlossenheit der jeweiligen Betreiber, Hand in Hand mit der einheimischen Bevölkerung und unter dem Gebot des Naturschutzes zu arbeiten.

› **ccafrica.com**
Mit 30 privaten Luxushütten, die über Südafrika, Kenia, Tansania, Zimbabwe, Namibia und Botswana verteilt liegen, gehört die Conservation Corporation Africa zu den größten afrikanischen Anbietern im Bereich des Ökotourismus. Ein Unternehmen mit Schwerpunkt auf geführten Wandersafaris, das sich in Wort und Tat der Förderung Afrikas, seiner Natur und der Unterstützung seiner Bewohner verschrieben hat.

› **classicsafaris.com**
«The darkest thing about Africa has always been our ignorance of it»; spezialisiert auf alle möglichen Arten afrikanischer Safaris, darunter Großwild–Fotosafaris, Wander-, Reit-, Hausboot- und Heißluftballonsafaris sowie Tiefseefischen.

› **cobra-verde.de**
Die deutsche Website deckt ganz Afrika ab, von Norden nach Süden, darunter Marokko, Algerien, Gambia, Mali, Ghana, Senegal und Tunesien. Ein ausgeklügelter Tourenplaner mit sehr guten Informationen zu jedem Land, schönen Fotos und einer Auswahl an Unterkunftsmöglichkeiten.

› **eco-resorts.com**
Fördert kleine einzigartige, Camps und Lodges in Kenia, Ruanda und Tansania welche die lokale Gemeinschaft unterstützen und sich im Naturschutz engagieren.

› **experience-egypt.com**
Hervorragende Informationen zu Geschichte, Geographie und Kultur Ägyptens sowie zu Anreise und Touren. Eine ansprechend gestaltete Seite, die leicht zu navigieren ist.

› **africanhistory.about.com**
Commencez par ce site pour mieux connaître ce vaste continent dont nous sommes tous originaires. Il couvre de nombreux sujets, notamment l'archéologie, l'exploration, l'histoire politique et la chronologie.

› **africaadventures.com**
Safaris personnalisés et sur mesure « pour découvrir la véritable Afrique », que vous séjourniez dans un petit hôtel situé dans une réserve, que vous dormiez sous la tente dans un camp classique ou que vous soyez logé dans un petit ranch privé. Les sites proposés ont été choisis pour l'accueil chaleureux que vous réservent les propriétaires, pour la beauté du lieu et sa faune exceptionnelle et pour la contribution des établissements concernés à la protection de l'environnement et à l'amélioration des conditions de vie des populations locales.

› **ccafrica.com**
Conservation Corporation Africa, l'une des sociétés de tourisme écologique les plus respectueuses du potentiel, de la nature et des besoins de l'Afrique, dispose de 30 hôtels privés luxueux dans des réserves en Afrique du Sud, au Kenya, en Tanzanie, au Zimbabwe, en Namibie et au Botswana.

› **classicsafaris.com**
Ce site est géré par des consultants installés aux États-Unis et qui sont des spécialistes de tous les types de safaris en Afrique. Les propositions sont adaptées à tous les calendriers, à tous les styles et à toutes les bourses.

› **cobra-verde.de**
Ce site en allemand traite de toute l'Afrique, du nord au sud, notamment le Maroc, l'Algérie, la Gambie, le Mali, le Ghana, le Sénégal et la Tunisie. Il organise des circuits dans le moindre détail et propose de nombreux renseignements sur chaque pays, de belles photos et une sélection d'hôtels.

› **eco-resorts.com**
Ce site fait la promotion de petits camps et hôtels uniques situés en Afrique orientale, plus précisément au Kenya, au Ruanda et en Tanzanie, qui s'impliquent dans l'aide aux communautés locales et la protection de l'environnement.

› **experience-egypt.com**
Informations très intéressantes sur l'histoire, la géographie et la culture égyptienne et sur les transports et les circuits. Ce site bien conçu, attrayant et d'une navigation facile propose également des liens.

TASCHEN Web Picks: Join the great tradition of explorers – Ibn Battuta, David Livingstone, Henry Morton Stanley, Mary Kingsley, Mungo Park, René Caillié, Heinrich Barth, Richard

› **getawaytoafrica.com**
The website of *Getaway* magazine; hundreds of destinations and accommodations, guides, advisories, news and travel packages. Offers a wide range of exclusive trips researched by Getaway's travel journalists. In-depth country guides, features on what to do and where to go, with links to other useful websites.

› **go2africa.com**
Features 1,500 safari lodges, hotels, and guest houses in Southern & East Africa. Feature Articles, travel ideas and tips, and country specifics.

› **gonomad.com**
For unconventional travel ideas, places you can go and make a positive contribution to, articles and top picks for places to stay in Africa, from eco-lodges to retreats.

› **greenwoodguides.com**
Special handpicked accommodation with links to the places recommended. For 'independent travellers who want to explore the country, avoid the tourist hordes, discover hidden places and meet interesting people in the process. In concert with an annually published guidebook.

› **hiptravelguide.com**
The 'hip travel' guide has 'scoured the net for the best Morocco sites'. Chatty and informative with a different point of view, photos and great links to some other intriguing sites.

› **i-escape.com**
Detailed and very good information on hideaways, including who goes there, what the food's like, the highs and lows, with photos, prices and direct links to each place

› **responsibletravel.com**
"Holidays that give the world a break": a diversity of pre-screened trips and accommodation provided by leading tour operators, accommodation owners and grass roots community projects. In time, responsible will be to travel what organic is to food – a consumer favourite that is better for you, better for local communities, and better for the planet.

› **safarinow.com**
The largest online trading platform of guesthouses, B&Bs, hotels, safari-lodges and tour providers in Africa. Focus is on Southern Africa, with links to individual places to make direct bookings.

› **getawaytoafrica.com**
Die Webseite des Magazins »Getaway«; bietet Hunderte von Reisezielen und Unterkunftsmöglichkeiten, Führer, Ratgeber, Nachrichten und Reiseangebote. Viele exklusive Trips, recherchiert und aufbereitet von »Getaway« - Reisejournalisten. Links zu anderen nützlichen Webseiten.

› **go2africa.com**
Nimmt 1.500 Safari-Lodges, Hotels und Pensionen im Süden und Osten Afrikas unter die Lupe. Hintergrundartikel, Reisevorschläge und -tipps, sowie Informationen zu den einzelnen Ländern.

› **gonomad.com**
Unkonventionelle Reisen, mit denen man einen sinnvollen Beitrag zum wirtschaftlichen Aufbau der jeweiligen Ortschaft leisten kann. Artikel und Geheimtipps zu Unterkunftsmöglichkeiten, die von der Öko-Lodge bis zum Verwöhnhotel reichen.

› **greenwoodguides.com**
Besondere, handverlesene Unterkünfte. Gedacht für Reisende, die dem Massentourismus aus dem Weg gehen und stattdessen lieber die verborgenen Winkel des Landes erkunden und dabei interessante Menschen kennenlernen möchten.

› **hiptravelguide.com**
Der Hip Travel Guide hat das Internet nach den sehenswertesten Plätzen Marokkos durchforstet. Unterhaltsame und informative Darstellung aus einem neuen Blickwinkel, mit Fotos und Links zu anderen faszinierenden Seiten.

› **i-escape.com**
Detaillierte Informationen zu abseits der Touristenpfade liegenden Orten; beschreibt auch die Küche sowie Plus- und Minuspunkte, mit Fotos, Preisen und direkten Links zu jeder Unterkunft.

› **responsibletravel.com**
»Holidays that give the world a break«: eine Vielfalt ausgewählter Touren und Unterkünfte, bereitgestellt von verschiedenen Reiseanbietern, Hotelbesitzern und Gemeinschaftsprojekten.

› **safarinow.com**
Umfangreichste Onlineplattform für Pensionen, Garnis, Hotels, Safari-Lodges und Reiseanbieter in Afrika. Der Schwerpunkt liegt auf Südafrika, mit Links zu einzelnen Hotels, die eine direkte Buchung möglich machen.

› **getawaytoafrica.com**
Le site du magazine « Getaway » propose des centaines de destinations et d'hôtels, des guides, des conseils, des actualités et des voyages organisés ainsi qu'un grand choix de voyages uniques sélectionnés par les journalistes de « Getaway ».

› **go2africa.com**
Ce site répertorie 1.500 hôtels spécialisés dans les safaris et autres hôtels et pensions de famille en Afrique méridionale et orientale. Articles de fond, idées de voyages, conseils et spécificités des pays.

› **gonomad.com**
Des idées de voyages originales pour partir en vacances tout en apportant votre contribution au lieu visité. Ce site contient des articles et propose les meilleurs points de chute en Afrique, depuis les hôtels écologiques jusqu'aux refuges.

› **greenwoodguides.com**
Ce site propose une sélection de logements triés sur le volet et des liens vers les hôtels recommandés. Il est destiné aux « voyageurs qui souhaitent explorer le pays pour rencontrer des gens intéressants et éviter les hordes de touristes ».

› **hiptravelguide.com**
Le guide du « voyage branché » a « passé Internet au crible pour y trouver les meilleurs sites sur le Maroc ». Vivant et regorgeant d'informations, il émet un point de vue original et propose des photos et des liens très intéressants vers d'autres sites surprenants.

› **i-escape.com**
Ce site fournit des informations détaillées sur certains lieux de retraite. Il décrit la qualité de la restauration, les points positifs et négatifs et accompagne ces renseignements de photos, de tarifs et de liens directs vers chaque hôtel mentionné.

› **responsibletravel.com**
Une sélection des meilleurs voyages et logements proposés par des voyagistes de premier plan, des propriétaires et des projets communautaires populaires.

› **safarinow.com**
La plus importante plate-forme commerciale en ligne en matière de pensions de famille, de bed and breakfast, d'hôtels, d'hôtels-safari et d'organisateurs de circuits en Afrique. Ce site propose également des liens vers les hôtels évoqués.

Francis Burton, Vasco da Gama – in an exploration of the African continent, but in the comfort of your own cyberspace. Just add www. to these addresses and discover Africa...

› **safari-portal.de**
"The leading internet directory for travel in East Africa and southern Africa". In German and English; with thousands of links to country information, travel guides, vaccine recommendations, accommodation, safari and tour operators, car rental services, and more. Plus virtual safaris, with web-cams.

› **southafrica-travel.net**
South Africa specific, also a sister site in German, attractions, history, geology, people, wildlife travel destinations accommodation with direct links; very informative.

› **taschen.com**
To explore books to escape into and with, on hundreds of subjects; from Africa to Asia to America, advertising to architecture, Marilyn Monroe to Muhammad Ali, wrestling to wildlife, to the universe and underwear.

› **ultimateafrica.com**
USA based safari experts, includes tailor-made and group safaris. Hands-on knowledge, personal recommendations, and information about what to expect. Pay the same as booking direct with African lodges, camps, airlines, and group tour operators.

› **unchartedoutposts.com**
Diverse safari properties in Africa; private ranches, small intimate lodges and stylish tented camps. These properties are mostly individually owned and operated by individuals devoted to preserving the wilderness and the culture of the local people.

› **wildwatch.com**
Part of the CC Africa site, with articles and news about conservation, community activities, and wildlife, interestingly written. For example, "The leopard, often called the 'Prince of Darkness', is identical in proportion and shape to a domestic cat – just much bigger."

› **zambezi.com**
A "scenic guide" to safaris in Zimbabwe, Zambia, Botswana and Namibia, including descriptions, maps, photo galleries, links to camps, lodges, and individual operations. Traditional safaris and adventure travel, such as canoeing and riverboarding – "as Hawaii is to surfing so the Zambezi is to riverboarding".

›**safari-portal.de**
»Das führende Internetportal für Reisen in Ost– und Südafrika«, auf Deutsch und Englisch. Enthält Tausende von Verweisen zu Länderinfos, empfohlenen Impfungen, Reiseführern, Unterkunftsmöglichkeiten, Safari– und Reiseanbietern, Mietwagenfirmen und vielem mehr. Mit virtuellen Safaris und Webkameras.

› **southafrica-travel.net**
Spezialisiert auf Südafrika, mit deutscher Version, thematisiert Sehenswürdigkeiten, Geschichte, Geologie, Bevölkerung und Safariunterkünfte mit direkten Links; Ausgesprochen informativ!

› **taschen.com**
Bücher, in die Sie ein- und abtauchen können, ideal als Reisebegleiter. Wählen Sie unter Hunderten von Themen: von Afrika über Asien bis Amerika, vom Anzeigenentwurf bis zur Architektur, von Marilyn Monroe bis Muhammad Ali, von Ringen bis Raubtier, vom Universum bis zur Unterwäsche.

› **ultimateafrica.com**
Safariexperten mit Sitz in den USA. Maßgeschneiderte und Gruppensafaris. Persönliche Empfehlungen und Informationen darüber, was Sie vor Ort erwartet. Gleicher Preis wie bei Direktbuchung von Lodges, Camps, Flügen oder über Anbieter von Gruppenreisen.

› **unchartedoutposts.com**
Verschiedene Safariunterkünfte in Afrika; private Gutshöfe, kleine persönliche und stilvolle Zeltlager. Die meisten dieser Unterkünfte werden von Privatpersonen geführt, die sich allesamt dem Schutz der Tierwelt und dem Erhalt der einheimischen Kultur verschrieben haben.

› **wildwatch.com**
Teil der CC Africa Webseite mit Artikeln und Neuigkeiten zu Naturschutz, Förderprogrammen und Tierwelt. Interessant geschrieben, zum Beispiel: »The leopard, often called the Prince of Darkness, is identical in proportion and shape to a domestic cat – just much bigger«.

› **zambezi.com**
Ein Landschaftsführer für Safaris in Zimbabwe, Zambia, Botswana und Namibia mit Beschreibungen, Karten, Fotos und Verweisen zu Camps, Lodges und individuellen Anbietern. Klassische Safaris und Abenteuerreisen, wie Kanutouren und Riverboarding.

› **safari-portal.de**
Ce site en allemand et en anglais propose des milliers de liens vers des sites fournissant des informations sur les différents pays, des guides de voyage, des recommandations en matière de vaccin, des renseignements sur l'hébergement, sur les organisateurs de safaris et les voyagistes, sur les locations de voiture, etc. Vous pouvez également y voir des safaris virtuels par l'intermédiaire de web-cams.

› **southafrica-travel.net**
Spécialisé dans l'Afrique du Sud, ce site existe aussi en allemand. Il présente les attractions touristiques, l'histoire et la géologie du pays, ses habitants, l'hébergement sur les sites où l'on peut observer la faune et contient des liens directs. Très instructif.

› **taschen.com**
Évadez-vous en découvrant des livres que vous pourrez également emmener avec vous en vacances. Vous avez le choix entre des centaines de sujets, tels que l'Afrique, l'Asie, l'Amérique, la publicité, l'architecture, Marilyn Monroe, Mohammed Ali, la lutte, la faune, l'univers ou encore les sous-vêtements.

› **ultimateafrica.com**
Conçu par des experts en safari basés aux États-Unis, ce site présente des safaris sur mesure ou en groupe. Il contient des recommandations personnelles et des renseignements sur ce qui vous attend sur place.

› **unchartedoutposts.com**
Ce site présente diverses propriétés africaines spécialisées dans le safari : ranchs privés, petites pensions tranquilles et camps de toile chics. Dans l'ensemble, chacune de ces propriétés est gérée par des personnes privées qui se consacrent à la protection de l'environnement et à la préservation de la culture des communautés locales.

› **wildwatch.com**
Ce site fait partie du site de CC Africa. Articles et actualités sur la défense et la préservation de l'environnement ,le programme de développement communautaire et la faune. Le ton est original. Par exemple : « Les proportions et l'allure du léopard, souvent appelé "Prince des Ténèbres", sont analogues à celles d'un chat domestique, mais en beaucoup plus gros. »

› **zambezi.com**
« Guide panoramique » sur les safaris au Zimbabwe, en Zambie, au Botswana et en Namibie. Ce site comprend des descriptions, des cartes, des galeries de photos, des liens vers des camps et des hôtels et vers des centres d'hébergement. Il propose des safaris traditionnels et des voyages axés sur l'aventure, notamment des parcours en canoë kayac et du riverboarding.

TASCHEN Web-Tipps:
Tun Sie es den großen Entdeckern gleich – Ibn Battuta, David Livingstone, Henry Morton Stanley, Mary Kingsley, Mungo Park, René Caillié, Heinrich Barth, Richard Francis Burton, Vasco da Gama – erforschen auch Sie den afrikanischen Kontinent, jedoch mit all dem Komfort, der den virtuelle Raum bietet. Setzen Sie einfach www. vor die folgenden Adressen und lernen Sie Afrika kennen...

Les meilleurs sites web selon TASCHEN :
Partez sur les traces des grands explorateurs – Ibn Battuta, David Livingstone, Henry Morton Stanley, Mary Kingsley, Mungo Park, René Caillié, Heinrich Barth, Richard Francis Burton, Vasco de Gama – et découvrez le continent africain grâce à Internet en restant confortablement assis devant votre ordinateur. Ajoutez www à ces adresses et découvrez l'Afrique...

Photo Credits | Fotonachweis
Crédits photographiques

The published information, addresses and pictures have
been researched with the utmost care. However, no
responsibility or liability can be taken for the correctness
of the details. The information may be out of date due to
current changes. In such cases, please refer to the rele-
vant websites for current prices and details.

Die veröffentlichten Informationen, Adressen und Bilder
sind mit größter Sorgfalt recherchiert. Dennoch kann für
die Richtigkeit keine Gewähr oder Haftung übernommen
werden. Die Informationen können durch aktuelle
Entwicklungen überholt sein. Bitte entnehmen Sie den
jeweiligen Websites die derzeitigen Preise und Angaben.

Bien que nous ayons recherché avec soin les informations,
les adresses et les photos de cet ouvrage, nous déclinons
toute responsabilité. Il est possible en effet que les don-
nées mises à notre disposition ne soient plus à jour.
Veuillez vous reporter aux différents sites web pour obtenir
les prix et les renseignements actuels.

© 2009 TASCHEN GmbH
Hohenzollernring 53, D-50672 Köln
www.taschen.com

ORIGINAL EDITION:	© 2003 TASCHEN GmbH
CONCEPT AND LAYOUT:	Angelika Taschen, Cologne
PROJECT MANAGER:	Stephanie Bischoff, Cologne
LITHOGRAPH MANAGER:	Thomas Grell, Cologne
EDITORIAL COORDINATION:	Julia Krumhauer, Cologne
TEXT EDITED:	LocTeam, S.L., Barcelona
GERMAN TRANSLATION:	Sylvia Still for LocTeam, S.L., Barcelona
FRENCH TRANSLATION:	Stéphanie Tabone for LocTeam, S.L., Barcelona
DESIGN:	Lambert und Lambert, Düsseldorf
PRINTED IN	China
ISBN	978-3-8365-1499-6

To stay informed about upcoming TASCHEN titles, please
request our magazine at www.taschen.com/magazine or
write to TASCHEN, Hohenzollernring 53, D-50672 Cologne,
Germany; contact@taschen.com; Fax: +49-221-254919. We
will be happy to send you a free copy of our magazine,
which is filled with information about all of our books.